salt to taste

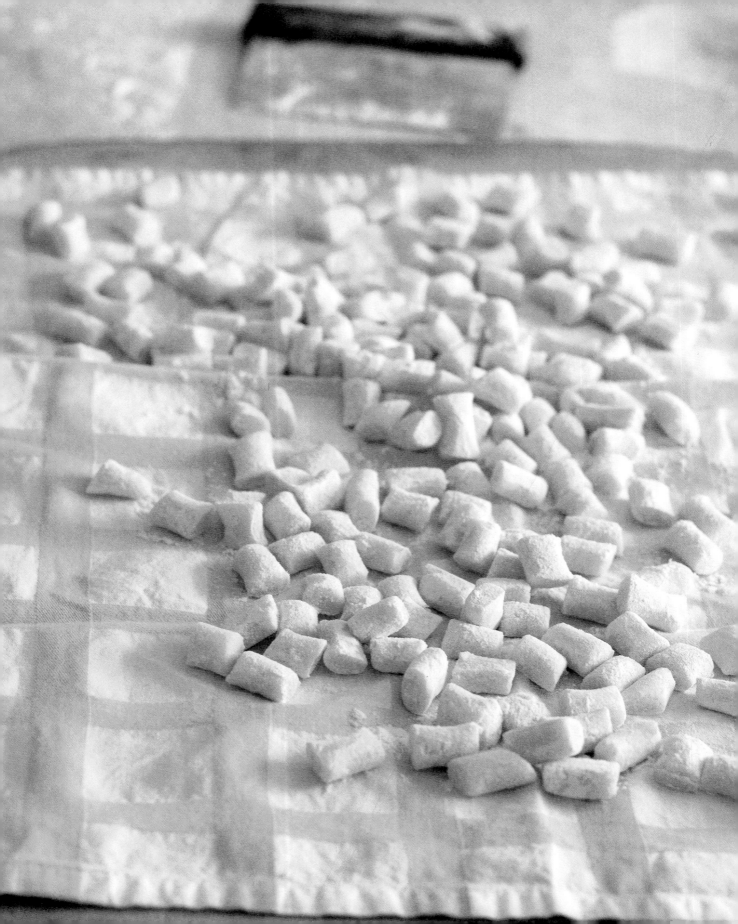

salt to taste

THE KEY TO CONFIDENT, DELICIOUS COOKING

MARCO CANORA

with Catherine Young

Photographs by John Kernick

Foreword by Tom Colicchio

RODALE

© 2009 by Marco Canora

Photographs copyright © 2009 by John Kernick

Rodale books may be purchased for business or promotional use or for special sales. For information, please write to:
Special Markets Department, Rodale Inc., 733 Third Avenue, New York, NY 10017

Printed in the United States of America

Rodale Inc. makes every effort to use acid-free ⊗, recycled paper ♻.

Book design by Christina Gaugler

Library of Congress Cataloging-in-Publication Data
Canora, Marco.
   Salt to taste : the key to confident, delicious cooking / Marco Canora with Catherine Young.
     p.   cm.
   ISBN-13 978–1–59486–780–4 hardcover
   ISBN-10 1–59486–780–1 hardcover
  1. Cookery, Italian. 2. Salt. I. Young, Catherine. II. Title.
   TX723.C28324 2009
   641.9545—dc22   2009020051

Distributed to the trade by Macmillan

2 4 6 8 10 9 7 5 3 1 hardcover

We inspire and enable people to improve their lives and the world around them
For more of our products visit **rodalestore.com** or call 800-848-4735

To my wife, Amanda; my daughter, Stella;
my mom, Laura; and my aunt, Leda

contents

foreword

when Marco arrived at Gramercy Tavern in the winter of
1996, he had a long ponytail down his back, a scanty resume, and good
hands, which is chef shorthand for the knack, the touch, whatever you
want to call it. I could see by the way he worked with food that he had
that indefinable *something* all great cooks need in order to go places.

He also had the kind of passion for the craft that can't be taught—
you either have it or you don't. I remember Marco's first few weeks on
the line: He would trot down to the pass at every opportunity to watch
as food was plated and then scurry back to his pans without missing a
beat. He wasn't just talented, he was curious, an unbeatable
combination.

Marco told us about how he'd grown up cooking with his mother and
aunt from a time before memory. The ease and pleasure with which those
two fine Tuscan cooks met each meal had made its way deep into his
consciousness, and soon Marco was my sous chef, running a tight ship
and thinking on his feet. It was a measure of Marco's worth to me that I
released him each summer to chef at his mother's excellent trattoria on
Martha's Vineyard. I wanted him to get used to running his own kitchen
for selfish reasons—the idea for a new restaurant was percolating, and I
knew Marco could be invaluable there as chef de cuisine.

Marco spoke longingly of Italy and his desire to learn at Fabio
Picchi's famous Cibrèo, known for its inventive take on ancient

Florentine cuisine. Happily, we had a connection there and were able to send him for a *stage* in 1998. Marco came back from Florence transformed in a subtle but important way; whereas the cooking at Gramercy Tavern derived from the French techniques—stocks, sauces, butter—Cibrèo brought Marco back to his Tuscan roots—vegetables, olive oil, soffritto.

At Cibrèo, the lessons Marco learned in his mother's kitchen were cemented and refined. For the restaurant that was to become Craft, I was hankering for simple roasts and clearer flavors, and Marco understood instinctively what I meant; whereas most chefs would have been afraid of simplicity, Marco embraced it. Food that precise—uncomplicated, yet complex—required a chef of the highest confidence and skill, which he was.

Cooking for many chefs is a job. But for Marco, cooking is a lifestyle. He cooks at home, much to the enjoyment of family and their wide circle of friends. This book reflects that multidimensionality—by nature, cooking at home is different than that done in a restaurant, but it comes from the same place: true passion, knowledge and love of fine ingredients, and a conviction that one should do only as much to a dish as it needs to be great, never more. Marco Canora cooks with his heart and soul. He cooks what he likes to eat. He's interested in tradition but is never dogmatic about it, finding inventive ways to refer to the past with one foot firmly planted in the modern world. The recipes in this book are as much of a joy to prepare as to devour. May you use it to cook often and eat well.

Tom Colicchio

introduction

when most people watch me salt a pot of boiling water for the first time, their reaction is disbelief. To them, the handfuls of Diamond Crystal kosher I dump in before adding pasta or vegetables seem excessive. What they don't realize is that a healthy dose of salt is essential to bringing out the natural flavors of almost any ingredient you can think of, and adding salt to water is actually a subtle way to season food, because it absorbs only a small amount of the salt as it is boiled or blanched.

Salt is a critical ingredient in every dish I make. Too much salt, however, can make any dish inedible. The obvious question then is how much is enough and how much is too much? I "salt to taste," but I want to stress that there are a few basic things you should know in order to follow my lead. You need to consider the flavor of all of your ingredients. Some foods are inherently salty—Parmesan cheese, for example, has a lot of salt in it, so if you are using significant amounts, you won't need as much salt. The same goes for anchovies. You also need to think about what happens to the salinity of a liquid as it cooks. A sauce that simmers away on the stove for hours will get saltier as the water evaporates and the flavors concentrate; the same thing happens with soups and braises. You need to be careful not to add too much salt in the early phases of cooking. Generally speaking, the best way to determine the perfect amount of salt is to add a little at a time, tasting as you go so that you can decide when no more is needed.

The phrase "salt to taste" isn't a one-time instruction; in fact, you could say the phrase "salt to taste" represents my overall approach to cooking. Great food is not the product of sticking rigidly to exact measurements. The best cooks I know rely mainly on their senses; they taste, smell, listen, and watch what they are cooking in order to determine what is needed to achieve the effect they want. They allow the food and stove to guide them rather than vice versa. If you are cooking a duck breast on the stovetop, for example, notice how it behaves when it reaches a perfect medium-rare: You'll find that it puffs up like a balloon and springs back when you poke it with your finger. Noticing changes as you go is what becoming a good cook is all about. It's about learning to sense when the meat has reached 125°F without repeatedly sticking it with a thermometer. (Besides, poking holes in the meat is not a good thing, because all of the delicious juices will flow out and leave you with a dry, tasteless piece of duck jerky.) This may take 8 minutes on my stove and 11 minutes on yours.

I've tried to sketch out recipes in a way that gives you a sense of what to look, listen, and feel for. In each instance, I've tried to spell out exactly what you need to know to get the best results. You might find that some relatively simple dishes are accompanied by more text than you expect. Don't be put off by this. I often hear from home cooks that chefs take too much culinary knowledge for granted when they write recipes, and it's true many of the assessments and adjustments chefs make as they prepare a dish are so ingrained after years behind a stove that we are unaware we are making them. In writing this book, I've made a conscious effort to take a step back and *really* examine how I approach what I do. These extra details are intended to help build your confidence and let you know when you are nailing a particular technique. I think you'll find that after you've made a dish a couple of times, you won't need to refer to more than the bare bones of each procedure, because you'll be comfortable *feeling* your way through the steps.

About 10 years ago, I spent some time working with Fabio Picchi, the chef and owner of Cibrèo, a well-known restaurant in Florence. To this day, the man remains a huge influence on my approach to cooking. Even though he didn't speak a word of English and my Italian was limited to proper nouns, most of them food related, I learned a lot from him. In the restaurant, he spent his day tasting. As the cooks finished each dish, they would put a small portion on a plate and bring it to Fabio. He would take a bite, and then if he was not completely satisfied (which he never was), he would tell the disappointed cook to go back and add more salt or stock or vinegar or whatever he felt was needed. This back and forth would go on at least three or four times before Fabio decided a dish was done. These cooks were experienced guys—the "problems" with what they made almost always came down to matters of taste, and Fabio trusted his own. Cibrèo was his restaurant, and the food was a reflection of his palate and no one else's. To me, that confidence is what good cooking is all about.

While trying out the recipes on the following pages, let your preferences be your guide. If you're not a fan of rosemary, substitute sage, thyme, or some other herb that you like. If a spicy kick is not your thing, leave the peperoncini or red pepper flakes out of the clams casino or use half the recommended amount. When all is said and done, I think tastebuds are far more reliable than measuring spoons when it comes to determining the right ratios of spice and seasoning for whatever dish you are making.

I know a lot of chefs like Fabio, who are great cooks (after all, I worked with Tom Colicchio for many years), but I also know great cooks who are not chefs. My mom and her older sister, Zia Leda, never worked in restaurants. The two of them probably taught me more about cooking than anyone else. I have always been in awe of how they can take the most humble ingredient, like the plastic-wrapped cauliflower sitting around in the produce section of the local supermarket, and transform it into something delicious. They taught me how to coax intense flavors from every ingredient I use, always by feeling and tasting my way through the cooking.

When I tell people what I ate as a child, many assume that my mother spent all day in the kitchen cooking. In fact, she was a single parent running her own interior design company, and yet she found time to cook healthy and delicious meals almost every night of the week. She cared deeply about her kids, and she wanted us to eat real food, not processed junk from the grocery store. (I can remember begging her, in the aisles of Grand Union, to buy me Oreos and Apple Jacks, all the tasty things my friends got to eat every day. She never did, and I am eternally grateful.) How did she pull it off? Her secret wasn't superhuman power or even excess energy. She just had a mix of efficiency, organization, and know-how that she picked up as a kid growing up in Tuscany. She also shopped smart, prepared what she could ahead of time, and picked recipes that suited her circumstances.

One thing my mom did that made life easier was to block out time each week and prepare large batches of a few key things. On Sundays, she might make a big pot of sauce or stew. She'd also make sure she had a few quarts of homemade broth stockpiled. In restaurants, we have to take this idea of prepping ahead to extremes, but it's smart to use the same principle at home. Starting the work week with your pantry and refrigerator well stocked, already having given some thought to what you're going to eat, is an old-fashioned approach to cooking, but it's also the best way I know to feed yourself well. My mom and my aunt couldn't have imagined any other way to feed their families; unfortunately, most of us today can. Cooking at home every day doesn't have to be an ordeal if you prepare a little. The best part is that the food you make stands a good chance of being cheaper and better for you than what you will find on most restaurant menus. Once you've honed your skills, you'll probably discover that what you make actually tastes better than what you'd get anywhere else.

If I can leave you with one last piece of advice, it is this: Cooking is not a mere chore but a creative outlet and a pastime, one that requires you to use all your senses, your intuition, and your resourcefulness. Don't be afraid to experiment and learn to accept the fact that sometimes your experiments will flop. Take the occasional failure with a grain of salt (so to speak) and learn from your mistakes. Start to think of the recipes in the pages that follow as templates, with information that you can apply to a wide variety of dishes, foods, and cooking situations, and this book will have served its purpose. If the food you are inspired to make brings smiles and satisfaction to those who eat it, then you will be doing something to make this crazy world we live in a better, more hospitable place.

stocking
the shelves

cooking food at home every day doesn't have to be stressful. No small part of success is having the right ingredients on hand, and by ingredients I don't mean just the meat and vegetables but also the spices, herbs, and condiments that make things taste good and simplify your work. When I was growing up, our pantry was always filled with canned tomatoes, tomato paste, olive oil, vinegar, bread crumbs, flour, pasta, rice, olives, anchovies, capers, dried herbs, spices, garlic, and beans. Our refrigerator was stocked with milk, eggs, cheese, and fresh herbs, not to mention onions, carrots, celery, and other vegetables that keep well. When my mother got home, she could make a veal cutlet with a quick pan sauce, or even simpler still, penne with Parmesan cheese, sage, and black pepper with a salad, and have dinner on the table in 30 minutes.

Years of restaurant work have taught me to take things a step further. Having brodo (meat broth—Easter Broth, page 8) and soffritto (aromatic flavoring base, page 10) on hand as well as marinated peppers, cooked beans, pickled onions, salsa verde, and lemon confit allows you to elevate everyday cooking without investing any extra time.

Start by going to the store and getting the basics. The list below covers a few essentials that I thought worth a few words. It's not intended as a complete shopping list, just a place to begin. Start here and fill your refrigerator, freezer, and cupboards wisely, and I think you'll find yourself cooking more easily and eating good food more often.

Salt I am not a salt connoisseur. Truth is I use Diamond Crystal kosher salt both at home and in the restaurant. It's really all you need. If you want to get fancy, splurge on fleur de sel for finishing salads and sprinkling over grilled and roasted meat.

Pepper I *am* finicky about pepper. It *must* be freshly ground. Buy a pepper mill and use it.

Nutmeg Another spice you should always buy whole is nutmeg. I use freshly grated nutmeg in pasta fillings and polpettone (page 13), and it makes all the difference.

Peperoncini Peperoncini are small, very hot dried Italian peppers that I use a lot. They have intense heat and complex flavor. Usually I mince peperoncini before I use them (mixing in a drop of oil as you chop makes the job easier and

neater). If you can't find peperoncini locally, they are available by mail.

Oregano Sicilian oregano is my choice. It's available by mail and at gourmet stores. This seasoning lends an authentically Italian flavor to many dishes. The oregano buds come dried on the stem. You can either crumble them off as needed (rubbing the buds in your fingers releases their flavor) or take a few minutes and crumble the whole package and store the oregano ready for use in a sealed container.

Tomatoes Canned San Marzano tomatoes are what I reach for all year long, except at the height of our local tomato season. They are harvested when perfectly ripe and are very flavorful.

Anchovies I always have salted anchovies packed in oil in my cupboard. I like to buy the jars, because once you open them you can twist the top back on and keep them in the refrigerator more or less forever. Tubes of anchovy paste are more expensive, but they are compact and tidy and again they keep.

Capers I like smallish capers packed in brine and always have an open container to dip into in my refrigerator to add to pastas, salads, and sandwiches as well as a backup in the pantry.

Olives Niçoise olives are tasty and salty but not overwhelming. I use them a lot to flavor sauces and braises. If you prefer other black olives, such as Kalamata, keep those on hand instead.

Pasta When I am at the supermarket, I buy De Cecco or Barilla. At the restaurant, I like to use a few harder-to-find brands: Setaro, Rustichella d'Abruzzo, and Martelli.

Olive Oil The flavors of olive oils vary depending on where they come from. Tuscan and Umbrian oils are grassy and peppery, while southern Italian oils are fruitier and softer on the palate. I tend to prefer Tuscan oil because that is what I grew up with, but personal taste should be your guide. You need a nice bottle of extra virgin to pour over food just before serving; use a less expensive extra virgin oil for sautéing. Virgin olive oil comes from the second press, pure olive oil from the third, and pommace from the fourth. When you are frying, oil from later presses is fine. A blend of olive oil and vegetable oil is a good way to go for deep-frying. Keep in mind that the flavor of olive oil fades with age, so young oil is more vibrant.

Vinegar I use red and white wine vinegars, sherry vinegar, and occasionally distilled vinegar. While I don't think you have to buy fancy wine vinegar, I do think it is essential to buy real aged balsamic. Avoid supermarket varieties; they are sweetened, artificially colored impostors at worst and young, commercially prepared knockoffs at best. Real aged balsamic is amazing stuff. It is sweet and tart, not sour, and should generally be drizzled on meats, salads, or fruit just before serving.

Parmigiano-Reggiano This is the one cheese you must have. It is the MSG of the Italian kitchen. It tastes nutty and salty and melts evenly, binding sauces and flavoring meatballs. A cow's milk cheese made in Emilia-Romagna, Parmigiano is aged a minimum of 12 months. Young cheese is fine for cooking, but look for cheese that is aged at least 3 years for grating over pasta or eating in chunks with a glass of wine.

Bread Crumbs Making bread crumbs is easy and the perfect way to use up old baguettes and loaves of country-style bread. Just break the stale bread into smallish pieces, then pulse them in a food processor. Store the bread crumbs in a sealed container in a dry place.

Broth Having good broth on hand is one of the best ways I know to lift up your cooking. Not only useful in soups, broth is an important ingredient in braises and many sauces. Easter Broth (page 8), a rich meat broth, is what I recommend. Good homemade chicken broth can be substituted. A little lighter tasting, homemade chicken broth will work even in recipes like Stracciatella (page 83), where the broth is the star. Commercial broth won't work in these featured roles, but good canned broth can be substituted in most braises and ragùs. My favorite canned broth is Health Valley Low Fat Chicken Broth.

Fresh Eggs The white of a fresh egg is thick and firm, the yolk a deep golden yellow, and the taste rich and wonderful. It is worth the trouble to seek out fresh eggs at a farmers' market.

pantry recipe: *eggs with tomato on toast*

4 eggs

¼ cup extra virgin olive oil

½ teaspoon thinly sliced garlic

Small pinch of minced peperoncini or red pepper flakes

½ teaspoon dried oregano, preferably Sicilian

5 canned tomatoes

Kosher salt and freshly ground black pepper

2 tablespoons chopped fresh basil

4 slices country white bread—whatever you have, toasted

Separate the eggs, reserving each yolk in its shell and combining 2 whites in a cup. Refrigerate the remaining 2 whites for another use.

In a cold medium skillet, combine the oil, garlic, peperoncini, and oregano. Turn on the heat and warm over medium-high heat until the garlic begins to fry (without browning) and the mixture becomes fragrant, about 2 minutes.

Raise the heat to high, then use your hands to crush each tomato into the pan, allowing the juice to fall into the skillet. Season lightly with salt and pepper. Fry the tomatoes, continuing to break them up with the fork. Cook until they concentrate and no longer look watery, 2 to 3 minutes. Add the basil.

Lower the heat to medium and stir in the egg whites. Cook until the whites become opaque and firm, thickening the tomato sauce, about 1 minute.

Turn off the heat. Using the back of a spoon, make 4 indentations in the sauce, allowing a few inches around each. Slip an egg yolk into each indentation. Draw the sauce in from the edges of the pan around each of the yolks. Cover the skillet and leave it on the stove, heat off, until the yolks are just warmed through and beginning to set, about 3 minutes for runny yolks.

Gently spoon some sauce and a yolk onto each piece of toast and serve immediately. I find rubbing some olive oil on the spoon helps prevent breaking the yolk.

SERVES 4

equipment

I don't think you need a fancy stove to cook great meals, but I do think the right pots and a few essential tools really help. Opposite are some of the tools I have at home, none of them too fancy or expensive.

the building blocks: broth and soffritto

When I think about telling people how to cook the way I grew up eating, I always wind up coming back to a few preparations that serve as building blocks. Brodo, Italian meat broth, is among the most important. Easter Broth, as we called it, is a rich concentrated liquid made from simmering a pot full of mixed meats. It's the foundation for many of the soups, braises, and pastas I make today.

Brodo is not stock, but broth. Stock is made from simmering bones, and broth is made from simmering meat. The practical difference is that stock contains more gelatin and is therefore an easier starting place for sauces. Because broths are made with whole pieces of meat and poultry rather than bones, they usually have deeper, more complex flavor. Broths also tend to be less cloudy—the protein in the meats in the pot acts as a filter that clarifies the broth as it simmers, leaving you with a beautifully clear liquid. French cuisine relies heavily on stock, while Italian depends much more on broth.

So why did we call it Easter Broth? Although brodo is made before all holiday meals in my family, it plays a featured role at Easter. Stracciatella, Italian egg drop soup (page 83), is always the first course of Easter dinner. And stracciatella always begins with brodo. For me, the name and the taste just stuck.

brodo

Brodo is easy to make with ingredients from the supermarket. Start with a chicken. Put it whole in the pot, then add 2 pounds of beef stew meat on the bone and a turkey drumstick (or two wings). Cover the meat by about 4 inches with water (you'll need about 7 quarts in all) and bring it to a boil over high heat.

As soon as the broth boils, begin to "clarify" it, lowering the heat to medium and pulling the pot to one side of the burner so it's partially off the burner. This forces the broth to boil in an oval circuit from top to bottom, circulating all the liquid over and around the meat. As the broth circulates, the fat and other impurities in the broth float to the surface. What will you see when you look into the

pot? The broth will bubble along one side of the pot. The rest of the surface will look active but not be bubbling. Fat and scum will rise with the bubbles and settle on the top.

Skim every 5 minutes or so. Be finicky about how you do this. Dip the ladle into the broth near the center of the pot just deep enough to barely submerge the front edge. Then keep it still. A thin stream of fat and foamy broth will be drawn into the ladle. Do this a couple of times, then wait another 5 minutes and do it again, continuing until the brodo looks clear, about half an hour.

Once the broth is clear, add aromatic vegetables. Chop and then add 2 onions, ½ bunch of celery, and 3 carrots. Add a 12-ounce can of tomatoes, 1 teaspoon peppercorns, and ½ bunch of flat-leaf parsley and simmer the broth until it's flavorful, about 2 hours.

Strain the broth and discard the vegetables but not the meat. (In my mind, brodo is forever linked with polpettone, the fried morsels of minced meat that, in my family, give a second life to the chicken, beef, and turkey used to make the broth. For a recipe, see page 13.) You'll wind up with about 3½ quarts of broth that can be refrigerated or frozen.

Soffritto, aromatics minced and cooked in olive oil, is the foundation of Tuscan cooking. The deep, round flavors of Italian braises, stews, and sauces are born as the vegetables fry in a generous amount of oil. Like good broth, soffritto is an old-school Italian ingredient that's essential to my cooking today.

I divide the universe of soffritto in three: blond, amber, and dark—a reflection of how deeply the vegetables are browned—carrots, onions, and to a lesser extent celery are full of natural sugars that caramelize as they cook. The longer you cook the soffritto, the darker it becomes. Generally, mild dishes rely on a blond soffritto—vegetables cooked to the color of straw. For moderately assertive dishes, you'll want to use amber soffritto—vegetables cooked to the color of cream soda, and for rich meaty dishes, you'll want to begin with dark soffritto—vegetables cooked to the color of good chocolate.

Blond

Amber

Dark

The ratio of onions to celery and carrots (or fennel when you're working with seafood—see the recipe for Cacciucco on page 182) is always 2:1:1. Beyond that, there are few hard-and-fast rules. What you're making determines which additional flavorings are added to the soffritto. Dried hot peppers, oregano, and tomatoes are frequent additions, together and separately, as are rosemary, garlic, and wine. This flexibility may seem intimidating at first, but with a very little bit of experience, you'll see it's what makes cooking fun—and what you cook more varied and interesting.

I use blond soffritto as the base, altered as necessary, for a variety of dishes. Whether you make a lot or a little, you have to cut the vegetables small; the smaller the vegetables are cut, the better the soffritto's flavor. I mince the celery and carrots (or fennel) in a food processor, but unless your food processor blade is very sharp, get out the knife for the onions or they will become a juicy mess. When cooking soffritto, you must *fry* the vegetables, not sweat them. You need good strong heat, medium-high to high, and you need to adjust it as you cook so the oil is always sizzling and the liquids the vegetables release evaporate almost instantly.

blond soffritto base

For blond soffritto base, start with 1¼ cups of extra virgin olive oil. Get the oil hot, then add 4 cups minced onion, 4 cups minced celery, and 2 cups minced carrot (or fennel). At first you'll see a lot of steam. Don't worry about sticking at this point. Just give the vegetables an occasional stir to keep them cooking evenly. When you no longer see steam rising from the pot because most of the water in the vegetables has evaporated, start keeping a closer eye on things, stirring to keep the soffritto from sticking and burning. Once the water is gone, about 1 hour, the sugars in the vegetables will start to caramelize. This happens abruptly, and you'll find the color moves from light to dark fast, so pay attention and stir regularly.

This yields over 4 cups and will keep about a week in the refrigerator (but if you cover it with oil, it will keep in the fridge for months). It can be doubled or tripled without a problem.

I don't believe in wasting food, and for my money, making **polpettone** is the perfect way to give cooked meat and poultry a second life. These addictive croquettes are made from minced leftovers. At home, we make them whenever we make broth (see Easter Broth, page 8) so we wind up with a combination of turkey, chicken, and beef; a leftover roast is an equally good place to begin. I recommend that you chop the meat by hand; it's more work, but the results are moister. And when you make the mix, remember that polpettone contain a lot of Parmigiano, so go easy with the salt.

polpettone

To make about 20 polpettone, boil a medium Yukon Gold potato in salted water until it is soft. While the potato cooks, chop ½ cup of parsley leaves with the peels from 2 lemons (make sure to remove the pith), and 3 garlic cloves. Chop 4 tightly packed cups of boiled or roasted meat, then add the meat to the parsley mixture and mince everything together. Put the meat and parsley mixture in a bowl; add ¾ cup grated Parmigiano and 2 beaten eggs. Peel the potato, mash it with a fork, and add it to the bowl. Season the polpettone mix with a little salt and a lot of freshly ground black pepper. Add a little broth or water to hold the mixture together. Form the polpettone into small logs or meatballs. Fry them in small batches in olive oil over medium-high heat, turning to brown them on all sides. Drain on paper towels and serve warm.

pasta, gnocchi, and risotto

this chapter devoted to pasta begins with my favorite tomato sauces. I start here for several reasons. First, great sauce over pasta is delicious, a commonplace combination that can be amazing when everything is cooked just right. Second, by sharing several quite different tomato sauces, I want to open the door a little wider on the complexity of Italian cooking. And finally, I start a chapter on pasta with freestanding sauce recipes because if you want to cook strategically, working ahead when you have time so you can still eat healthy meals when you're pressed, making a big batch of sauce is as good a way to begin as any I can think of.

Pomarola, the most basic sauce, is essentially a tomato puree. Make pomarola only in season and use it as a sauce in its own right or as the starting place for more elaborate sauces. The rest of the sauces here can be made with canned tomatoes. If fresh tomatoes aren't perfectly sweet and juicy, you will get a better result with canned, because they're picked and processed at the height of the season.

As I've said, it makes sense to make sauce in big batches. Most of the cooking is passive, simmering over low heat, so making more is not a lot more work than making less. Do remember to stir the sauce from time to time. As the water evaporates and the sauce concentrates, the Amatriciana and the Bolognese in particular have a tendency to stick and ultimately scorch. If the bottom burns, it can ruin the taste of the whole pot, so if you find your sauce sticking, pour it into a fresh pot, watch your heat carefully, and stir frequently.

All of these sauces work on fresh or dried pasta and can be frozen, so stock your freezer. You'll have the beginnings of really easy but delicious weekday meals as well as a head start on showstopping dishes like Lasagne Verde Bolognese (page 56).

pomarola

MAKES ABOUT 1 QUART

Late in the summer is the time to make pomarola—pureed stewed tomatoes. Pomarola is so much better than the canned puree you see at the grocer's. My mother and aunt spend days each August "putting up" jars and jars for the winter. I don't do much canning, but this simple puree is such a good starting place for sauce, or just as is over pasta, that I always make a batch or two to extend the season as long as possible.

15 very ripe plum tomatoes, cut into quarters

1 small onion, peeled and chopped

1 celery stalk, chopped

1 carrot, peeled and chopped

2 garlic cloves, peeled and chopped

½ bunch of fresh basil

3 tablespoons extra virgin olive oil

Kosher salt

Put the tomatoes, onion, celery, carrot, garlic, basil, and oil in a large pot. Season with salt and bring to a simmer over medium heat. Adjust the heat so the pomarola maintains a gentle simmer and cook until the tomatoes soften and break apart, about 30 minutes. Pass the mixture through a fine- or medium-holed food mill. The pomarola can be canned, refrigerated, or frozen. It's also good warmed in olive oil and served as the simplest possible sauce for pasta.

tuscan tomato sauce

MAKES ABOUT 2½ QUARTS

This is my favorite all-purpose tomato sauce. It begins with a soffritto, which gives the sauce a complexity and sweetness I like.

¾ cup extra virgin olive oil

1 medium onion, peeled and minced

1 small carrot, peeled and minced

1 celery stalk, minced

3 garlic cloves, peeled and minced

¼ cup minced fresh flat-leaf parsley leaves

¼ cup minced fresh basil leaves

1 tablespoon fresh thyme leaves

4 (28-ounce) cans tomato puree

Kosher salt and freshly ground black pepper

If you have Blond Soffritto Base (page 12), heat 1½ cups, add the garlic and herbs, and cook for 5 minutes to blend the flavors. Add the tomato puree and proceed with the recipe.

Heat the oil in a large heavy-bottomed pot over medium-high heat. Add the onion, carrot, celery, garlic, parsley, basil, and thyme and fry the soffritto (it should sizzle), stirring occasionally at first, then more frequently as the mixture begins to reduce in volume. When the soffritto is beginning to stick and color, about 10 minutes, add the tomato puree.

Season the sauce with a little salt and pepper, stir, and bring to a simmer. Lower the heat and gently simmer the sauce, stirring occasionally, until the oil floats on the surface, at least 1 hour (the longer and slower you cook the sauce, the richer its flavor will be). Adjust the seasoning with salt and pepper and use immediately or cool the sauce and refrigerate for up to 1 week or freeze.

Don't oversalt. I season minimally, then adjust when I use the sauce.

variation: cauliflower and tomato sauce

Divide a head of cauliflower into florets and roughly chop them. Add the cauliflower to the soffritto when the vegetables begin to soften, after about 5 minutes. Finish cooking the soffritto, then add the tomato puree and simmer as described above.

rich tomato sauce

MAKES ABOUT 2 QUARTS

This is the tomato sauce to use when you are making Veal and Ricotta Meatballs in Tomato Sauce (page 222). It's finished with butter, making a smooth finish and light, warm color. I use a handheld blender to emulsify the butter into the sauce, but if you don't have one, a regular blender will work.

¼ cup extra virgin olive oil

4 garlic cloves, peeled and smashed

3 (28-ounce) cans whole peeled tomatoes

Kosher salt and freshly ground black pepper

6 tablespoons (¾ stick) unsalted butter

15 large fresh basil leaves, chopped

Combine the oil and garlic cloves in a large pot and cook over low heat until the garlic is fragrant, about 5 minutes.

Increase the heat to high and add the tomatoes and their juices, breaking them into the pan with your hands. Season with salt and pepper and bring the sauce to a boil. Lower the heat to medium and let the sauce simmer until the oil separates and floats on the surface, about 30 minutes. Remove the pan from the heat.

Be sure to incorporate the butter into the sauce off the heat. This avoids the risk that the butter will "break," leaving the sauce oily rather than silky.

Cut the butter into tablespoons, then emulsify it into the sauce using a handheld blender. Blend in the basil and adjust the seasoning with salt and pepper. Serve immediately or cool and refrigerate for up to 1 week or freeze.

amatriciana sauce

MAKES ABOUT 2 QUARTS

Meaty and a little spicy, this sauce is worth the trouble it takes. You'll notice that I keep my heat down and take my time with each step. This is how you get the best flavor. Expect the ground pork to render a significant amount of fat. You can leave it in for flavor as I do or skim it off when the sauce is done. Fiore Sardo, a Sardinian sheep's milk cheese, is wonderful grated over spaghetti with Amatriciana sauce in place of the more familiar Parmigiano. At Insieme, we use a smoked variety that is really delicious.

About 2 tablespoons extra virgin olive oil

6 ounces ground guanciale or pancetta

2 cups diced onions

Kosher salt and freshly ground black pepper

2½ tablespoons minced garlic

About ¼ teaspoon minced peperoncini or red pepper flakes

2 (28-ounce) cans tomato puree

Heat a skim of oil, about 2 tablespoons, in a large pot over medium heat. Add the guanciale or pancetta and cook, stirring frequently, until the meat is no longer pink, about 3 minutes.

Add the onions and stir, coating the onions with the fat in the pot. Season with salt and pepper and continue cooking, stirring occasionally, until the onions are soft and golden, about 10 minutes.

Add the garlic and peperoncini (use more or less, depending on how spicy you like your sauce) and cook, stirring occasionally, until the mixture is aromatic, about 10 minutes more.

Add the tomato puree, season with salt and pepper, and bring to a simmer. Lower the heat and gently simmer the sauce, stirring occasionally, until it reduces and thickens slightly, the flavors blend, and the fat floats to the surface, about 40 minutes. At this point, the sauce can be used immediately or cooled and refrigerated for up to 1 week or frozen.

Guanciale, cured pork jowl, is my first choice for this recipe, but pancetta or unsmoked bacon can substitute.

A food processor is not the perfect replacement for a meat grinder but will work in a pinch if you cut the pork into strips, then freeze it before processing. When the pork is frozen, the fat won't melt during processing, so the meat breaks into small pieces and the result is closer to grinding.

bolognese sauce

I use this sauce when I make Lasagne Verde Bolognese (page 56). It is, of course, also good on pasta, fresh or dried. Have your butcher grind the mortadella or do it yourself. If you don't have a meat grinder, cut it into chunks and then freeze it so it is firm, not rock hard; pulse it in a food processor. If you can't find mortadella, substitute pancetta.

If you have Blond Soffritto Base (page 12), heat 1½ cups, then add the garlic and follow the recipe from there.

4 tablespoons (½ stick) unsalted butter

¼ cup extra virgin olive oil

1 medium onion, peeled and minced

1 celery stalk, minced

1 carrot, peeled and minced

Kosher salt and freshly ground black pepper

2 garlic cloves, peeled and minced

1 pound ground beef

½ pound ground pork

⅓ pound mortadella, ground

⅓ cup tomato paste

2 cups whole milk

2 cups red wine

1 (28-ounce) can whole peeled tomatoes

About ¼ whole nutmeg

4 cups Easter Broth (page 8) or chicken broth

Combine the butter and oil in a large heavy pot over medium-high heat. Add the onion, celery, and carrot; season lightly with salt and pepper. Fry, stirring frequently, until the soffritto starts to soften and color, about 20 minutes.

Add the garlic. When it's fragrant and before it starts to brown, add the beef, pork, and mortadella; season again with salt and pepper. Cook, stirring occasionally, breaking up the clumps of meat with the back of your spoon. Cook until the meat is no longer pink and is beginning to brown, about 25 minutes. (The meat will release a lot of fat and moisture—don't fret, the liquid will evaporate and you can skim the fat if you like when the sauce is done.)

Stir in the tomato paste and cook until it darkens and concentrates, about 5 minutes. Add the milk and cook at a lively simmer, adjusting the heat if necessary. Simmer until the milk disappears into the meat, 10 to 15 minutes. Add the wine and simmer again until the pan is almost dry.

Break the tomatoes into the pan, allowing the juices within to fall into the sauce (discard the excess juice in the can). Grate the nutmeg into the sauce and add the broth. Mix well and bring the sauce to a gentle simmer, adjusting the heat if necessary. Cook, stirring occasionally, until the sauce reduces and the oil floats to the surface, about 3 hours. Skim some (but not all) of the fat— leave some for flavor. Serve immediately over fresh or dried pasta or cool and refrigerate for up to 1 week or freeze.

about pasta

If I were to give a single piece of advice about how to make pasta dishes taste more authentically Italian and just plain better, it would be this: Finish cooking the pasta in the sauce! Finishing pasta in the sauce gives it a chance to absorb flavor, and the starch the pasta releases into the sauce helps the sauce cling to the pasta. The end result is a dish that is unified and flavorful in a richer way.

Don't drain pasta in a strainer. Instead, before it reaches al dente, when it's flexible but still pretty chewy, use tongs, a slotted spoon, or a mesh spider to lift the spaghetti or whatever you're cooking directly from the water into the sauce. Starchy water clings to it and goes into the sauce. This helps ensure there is enough liquid in the sauce to finish cooking the noodles.

So how long should you cook pasta in the water and in the sauce? That depends completely on what kind you are cooking—commercial pasta must cook considerably longer than homemade, which needs to boil only until it floats. And certain shapes take longer than others; spaghetti takes more time than capellini, and farfalle takes longer than either. The brand and age of pasta also have an effect. So my best advice is to check frequently as you boil the pasta, more frequently once the noodles begin to bend. When they are flexible, start tasting. When they are almost but not quite where you want them, add them to the sauce. Until you get the hang of it, err on the side of under- rather than overcooking the pasta in the water—you can always add a little extra cooking water to the sauce and let it cook until it's right.

The other point worth making is that some sauces go best with homemade egg pasta and some with commercial pasta. Traditionally, in the agriculturally rich north of Italy, pasta contained eggs. The resulting dough, which is pliable and easy to work, was made at home daily. When cooked, egg pasta is silken, flavorful, and absorbent, a perfect match for the meaty game-rich ragùs and the cream- and butter-based sauces typical of the north. Because it is homemade, traditional egg pasta shapes tend to be relatively simple—wider and narrower noodles (think pappardelle and fettuccine).

homemade spaghetti

At my restaurant, I make my own spaghetti and other eggless pastas. The results are very good, but unless you enjoy a challenge, I don't encourage you to try it at home. The dough is hard to work with, and you need an imported extruder. When we have spaghetti and other semolina pastas at my house, I use imported Italian pasta. Setaro, a brand made in Naples, is excellent if you want to go beyond the very good imported brands available at most supermarkets. Setaro is made the old-fashioned way, pressed through a brass extruder, leaving the pasta with a slightly sandpapery exterior—perfect for grabbing sauce.

In the south of Italy, most pasta is made from hard wheat semolina flour and does not contain eggs. The pasta is well suited to drying, and the dough is difficult to work. It is now generally commercially prepared. Eggless pasta is less porous and rich than the pasta of the north. It is toothsome and hearty, the ideal foil for olive oil–based sauce. Commercial dried eggless pasta comes in a huge number of shapes. Smooth sauces tend to go with simpler shapes (think spaghetti), and chunkier sauces tend to go with pastas with nooks and crannies (think orecchiette).

The next few recipes call for eggless pasta. I suggest you buy dried for the Linguine with Clam Sauce (page 31) and Pasta e Fagioli (page 36), but if you want to change things up, you can use fresh egg pasta for the others—preferably your own homemade.

spaghetti with cherry tomato sauce

SERVES 4 TO 6

Adding the lemony gremolata to the spaghetti at the last moment wakes up the flavors of the cherry tomato "sauce" in an unexpected but wonderful way.

FOR THE GREMOLATA:

    1 large garlic clove, peeled

    Strips of peel from ½ lemon, white pith removed

    2 tablespoons fresh flat-leaf parsley leaves

FOR THE PASTA AND SAUCE:

    1 pound spaghetti

    6 tablespoons extra virgin olive oil

    4 small garlic cloves, peeled and thinly sliced

    Pinch of minced peperoncini or red pepper flakes

    2 tablespoons chopped fresh flat-leaf parsley

    2 pounds cherry tomatoes, stemmed and halved

    Kosher salt and freshly ground black pepper

    ½ cup freshly grated Parmigiano-Reggiano

The sauce is cooked just long enough to soften the tomatoes, not until they completely break down. This way, the tomatoes retain a shadow of their individuality while their concentrated juices pull together.

TO MAKE THE GREMOLATA: Chop the garlic, lemon peel, and parsley together until they are finely minced. Put the gremolata in a bowl and reserve it.

TO MAKE THE PASTA AND SAUCE: Bring a large pot of salted water to a boil. Add the pasta and cook, stirring occasionally, until it is not quite al dente.

The amount of time it will take to get the tomatoes to release their juices and then reduce and concentrate them will vary. Lower the heat if things are moving too fast and don't hesitate to add some of the pasta cooking water to loosen the sauce.

While the pasta cooks, combine the oil, garlic, peperoncini, and parsley in a large skillet. Let the garlic and parsley infuse into the oil over low heat. Swirl the pan every so often. As soon as the garlic begins to color, raise the heat to high and add the tomatoes. Season with salt and pepper and fry the tomatoes, stirring frequently, until they are soft and starting to fall apart, 3 to 5 minutes.

Lift the pasta out of the water and add it to the skillet with the tomatoes. Finish cooking the pasta in the sauce, tossing it frequently, about 2 minutes. Add the Parmigiano. Serve the pasta topped with gremolata.

penne with fresh tomato sauce

SERVES 4 TO 6

Like the previous recipe, this one is best made when tomatoes are at their peak. But I have to admit, both are still good made with out-of-season supermarket tomatoes; just let them sit on your windowsill until they ripen.

You don't have to peel the tomatoes, but I usually do. I core them, then dunk them in boiling water to loosen the skin. It peels off very easily then.

2 pounds ripe, juicy plum tomatoes

6 tablespoons extra virgin olive oil plus additional for serving

4 small garlic cloves, peeled and thinly sliced

Kosher salt and freshly ground black pepper

1 pound penne rigate, spaghetti, or other fresh or dried pasta

10 fresh basil leaves

Freshly grated Parmigiano-Reggiano

Peel the tomatoes if you like, then cut each in half crosswise and squeeze out the seeds. Roughly chop the tomatoes and reserve them.

Combine the oil and garlic in a large skillet. Put the pan on the stove and turn the heat to medium. Let the garlic infuse into the oil, swirling the pan to prevent the garlic from burning. As soon as the garlic begins to color, add the tomatoes and increase the heat to high.

The goal is to get the tomatoes to release their juices and concentrate those juices as quickly as possible—you want them to fry, not stew, but you also don't want to scorch the sauce. If the tomatoes are loaded with water, you will need to cook the sauce longer over higher heat. If, on the other hand, your tomatoes are dry and starchy, you'll need to work more slowly over more gentle heat.

Season with salt and pepper and fry the tomatoes over high heat, stirring frequently, until they are soft and beginning to fall apart. (The cooking time can vary considerably.) If you want, take the pan off the heat while you cook your pasta and then get the tomatoes hot again when the pasta is ready to go.

Bring a large pot of salted water to a boil. Add the pasta and cook, stirring occasionally, until it is almost al dente.

Lift the pasta out of the water and add to the skillet with the tomatoes. Toss to coat the pasta with sauce and cook over high heat until the pasta is al dente.

Remove the pan from the heat. Tear the basil leaves into small pieces and add them to the pasta. Adjust the seasoning and serve immediately topped with Parmigiano and a little extra virgin olive oil.

farfalle with pesto

SERVES 4 TO 6

Farfalle is a great pasta shape to pair with pesto. The twists and curves of the bows catch the sauce. It's hard to beat as is, but if you want something more substantial, do like the Genoese and add a cup of boiled, peeled, and quartered small potatoes and a cup of boiled, trimmed green beans to the pasta and sauce and mix gently. Adjust the seasoning and serve.

¼ cup pine nuts

3 cups tightly packed fresh basil leaves

½ cup freshly grated Parmigiano-Reggiano

2 garlic cloves, peeled and sliced

1 cup extra virgin olive oil

Kosher salt and freshly ground black pepper

1 pound farfalle

Put the pine nuts in a medium skillet and toast them over low heat, tossing frequently to prevent burning. Cook the pine nuts until golden, about 5 minutes, then set them aside to cool.

Transfer the pine nuts to a food processor and add the basil, Parmigiano, and garlic. With the processor running, gradually add the oil in a steady slow stream. Adjust the seasoning with salt and pepper. Put the pesto in a bowl large enough to hold the farfalle.

Bring a large pot of salted water to a boil over high heat. Add the pasta and cook, stirring occasionally, until it is al dente.

Lift the pasta out of the water and put it in the bowl with the pesto (adding a little extra pasta cooking water to loosen the sauce if necessary). Mix gently, adjust the seasoning with salt and pepper, and serve.

Pesto is obviously great on pasta, but it is also good mixed into Maionese (page 256) to make a cold sauce to serve with roasted fish. It is also very good spooned over Eggplant in a Bag (page 138).

Pesto can be refrigerated for up to 5 days. Although it goes against conventional wisdom, at home we freeze it, cheese and all.

spaghetti with shrimp

SERVES 4 TO 6

Every Italian seaside restaurant has a version of this dish. I flour the shrimp before I sauté them. The flour thickens the "sauce" just enough so each strand of spaghetti winds up coated. Wine and fresh lemon juice brighten the dish. You want to start the shrimp when the spaghetti is almost ready, because they cook fast—2 to 3 minutes—and they toughen if they're overcooked.

1 pound spaghetti

1½ tablespoons extra virgin olive oil

4½ tablespoons unsalted butter

1 pound small to medium shrimp, peeled and deveined

Kosher salt and freshly ground black pepper

About 1 cup all-purpose flour

2 tablespoons minced shallot or onion

1½ tablespoons minced garlic

¾ cup dry white wine

Juice of 1½ lemons

½ cup finely chopped fresh flat-leaf parsley

You often see this made with small Mediterranean shrimp, but medium to large shrimp are also very good; just cut them into pieces so you get a little shrimp with each bite of pasta.

Bring a large pot of salted water to a boil over high heat. Add the pasta and cook, stirring occasionally, until it is almost al dente, about 5 minutes.

While the pasta cooks, heat the oil and 1½ tablespoons butter in a large skillet over high heat.

Season the shrimp with salt and pepper, then dredge them in the flour. Shake off the excess and add the shrimp to the skillet. Cook, without stirring, until the first side of each shrimp firms, about 1 minute. Flip the shrimp and add the shallot or onion and garlic, swirling the pan so nothing burns.

Cook until the garlic is fragrant and the shrimp are opaque, about 1 minute. Add the wine and lemon juice. Swirl the pan until the shrimp are cooked through, about 30 seconds more, then reduce the heat to low. Swirl in the remaining 3 tablespoons butter, 1 tablespoon at a time.

When you begin to work in the butter, make sure there is liquid in the skillet or the emulsification will break and the "sauce" will become greasy rather than creamy. If the pan looks dry, add a little pasta cooking water.

Lift the pasta out of the water and add it to the skillet with the shrimp. Add the parsley. Raise the heat and toss the pasta until it is well coated. Remove the skillet from the heat and adjust the seasoning with salt, pepper, and more lemon juice if you like. Serve immediately.

linguine with clam sauce

SERVES 4 TO 6

At Insieme, we essentially have two menus in one. We offer contemporary Italian food, and because it's always been a dream of mine, we also serve very traditional dishes. This is our linguine con vongole, a Tuscan rather than southern Italian approach to this classic and the way I've made linguine with clams as long as I can remember. Starting with soffritto (made with fennel instead of carrots) gives the finished dish deep and bright flavors. The clams are steamed, then minced and added along with their broth. It's a little more work up front, but I think there's a real payoff at the table.

FOR THE CLAMS:

3 dozen littleneck clams

About 2 tablespoons extra virgin olive oil

2 shallots, peeled and sliced

3 garlic cloves, peeled and sliced

1 cup dry white wine

FOR THE PASTA AND SAUCE:

¼ cup extra virgin olive oil plus additional for serving

½ cup minced onion

¼ cup minced celery

¼ cup minced fennel

1 tablespoon minced garlic

Pinch of minced peperoncini or red pepper flakes

½ teaspoon dried oregano, preferably Sicilian

1 pound linguine

Kosher salt and freshly ground black pepper

½ cup finely chopped fresh flat-leaf parsley

This recipe is all about timing the cooking of the pasta and sauce. It's easier than it seems. You can make the soffritto and cook the clams ahead of time, so all you have to coordinate is finishing the sauce and cooking the pasta. In fact, you could add the clams and broth to the soffritto, then cook your pasta. Just be sure not to boil the sauce until you add the linguine or the clams will get rubbery.

If you have Blond Soffritto Base (page 12), heat 1½ cups, then add the garlic and follow the recipe from there.

(recipe continues)

TO MAKE THE CLAMS: Cover the clams with water and let them soak for about an hour.

Heat a skim of oil, about 2 tablespoons, in a large pot over medium heat. Add the shallots and garlic and cook, stirring frequently, until they soften, about 3 minutes.

Lift the clams out of the water (the sand they release will have settled to the bottom of the bowl—so lift, don't drain the clams) and add them to the pot. Pour in the wine, raise the heat to high, cover the pot, and cook until the clams open, about 5 minutes.

Transfer the clams to a clean bowl. Allow them to cool, then remove them from their shells; reserve the cooking juices. Chop the clams finely and set aside. Strain the juices through a very fine sieve or a coffee filter and reserve.

TO MAKE THE PASTA AND SAUCE: Heat the oil in a high-sided skillet, large enough to hold the pasta, over medium-high heat. Add the onion, celery, and fennel and fry, stirring frequently, until the vegetables soften, about 7 minutes.

Add the garlic, peperoncini, and oregano. Fry the soffritto, stirring frequently, until the garlic softens, about 3 minutes. (The recipe can be made ahead to this point, but the clams need to go in at the very last minute or they will overcook.)

Shortly before you're ready to serve, bring a large pot of salted water to a boil. Add the pasta and cook until it is not quite al dente—flexible but not yet done.

While the pasta cooks, add the clams and the reserved broth to the soffritto and season lightly with salt and pepper.

Lift the pasta out of the cooking water and add it to the clam sauce. Raise the heat to high and cook the pasta in the sauce, stirring frequently, until the pasta absorbs the sauce and is nicely al dente, 2 to 4 minutes. Add the parsley and adjust the seasoning with salt and lots of pepper. Serve drizzled with oil.

It is always a good idea, but it is essential in this recipe, that you finish cooking the pasta in the sauce. This is what makes the dish come together—literally. So make sure there is some liquid in the pan (add pasta water if you need to), and boil the linguine with the clams until the clam juices thicken enough to coat the pasta.

pantry recipe: penne with parmigiano, sage, and cracked black pepper

SERVES 4 TO 6

- 1 pound penne rigate
- 4 tablespoons (½ stick) unsalted butter, cut into pieces
- 1 heaping tablespoon chopped fresh sage
- About ½ cup freshly grated Parmigiano-Reggiano
- Kosher salt and freshly ground

Bring a large pot of salted water to a boil. Add the pasta and cook, stirring occasionally, until it is al dente. Put the butter in a mixing bowl. Add the sage and Parmigiano. Using a slotted spoon, lift the pasta out of the water and put it in the bowl (transferring the pasta with a spoon ensures that a little water clings to it, which helps to loosen the sauce; add a little more cooking water if you need to). Add several generous grindings of

rigatoni with cauliflower, pecorino, hot pepper, and bread crumbs

SERVES 4 TO 6

Because cauliflower is so hearty, we wind up seeing it (looking a little sad) sitting on the supermarket shelf more or less year round. It's easy to forget cauliflower is best eaten fresh and in season. When it is, it's one of my favorite vegetables. This boldly flavored pasta is a great way to showcase freshly picked cauliflower, but even made with that humble grocery store cauliflower, it will end up tasting quite delicious.

If you have Blond Soffritto Base (page 12), heat 1½ cups, add the garlic, and cook for 5 minutes to blend the flavors. Add the tomatoes and proceed with the recipe.

¼ cup extra virgin olive oil

½ cup minced onion

¼ cup minced carrot

¼ cup minced celery

3 garlic cloves, peeled and minced

1 large head of cauliflower, broken into small florets

Kosher salt and freshly ground black pepper

Large pinch of minced peperoncini or red pepper flakes

1 (28-ounce) can whole peeled tomatoes

1 pound rigatoni

½ cup chopped fresh flat-leaf parsley

½ cup grated pecorino cheese

¼ cup plain bread crumbs

3 tablespoons unsalted butter, melted

Heat the oil over medium-high heat in a large heavy-bottomed pot. Add the onion, carrot, celery, and garlic. Fry the soffritto, stirring often, until the vegetables soften, about 10 minutes.

Add the cauliflower and mix thoroughly. Season with salt, pepper, and peperoncini. Cook until the cauliflower begins to soften, about 5 minutes.

Break the tomatoes into the pot, allowing the juices within to fall into the sauce (discard the juice in the can). Mix well, reduce the heat to low, and simmer gently until the cauliflower is tender and begins to break apart, about 10 minutes. Season with salt and pepper.

Bring a large pot of salted water to a boil over high heat. Add the pasta and cook, stirring occasionally, until it is almost al dente. Lift the cooked pasta out of the water and add it to the cauliflower mixture to finish cooking in the sauce.

Add enough of the pasta cooking water to loosen the sauce, about ½ cup, and increase the heat to medium-high. Add the parsley and half of the pecorino and cook, stirring to coat the pasta with cauliflower sauce. When the pasta is al dente, remove the pot from the heat.

Meanwhile, preheat the broiler. In a small bowl, mix the bread crumbs, butter, and the remaining pecorino. Transfer the pasta and sauce to a shallow baking dish. Spoon an even layer of the bread crumbs over the pasta. Brown the bread crumbs under the broiler, about 3 minutes. Let the pasta rest for 5 minutes, then serve.

This recipe is also very good made with chopped fresh savoy cabbage, sliced zucchini, cubed eggplant, or broccoli florets instead of the cauliflower.

pasta e fagioli

I've had many versions of this dish over the years, and the thing that varies most is the consistency. I've had "fagioli" served as a thin broth with pasta, a hearty pasta dressed with a sauce of beans and puree, and almost everything in between. There's no right way. Use the puree, thinning or thickening it, to get things the way you want them. Personally, I like pasta e fagioli that's hearty—more a pasta dish than a soup. If you do too, follow the recipe as is; if not, add more broth. Either way, do add a little broth just before serving (the pasta and beans keep on absorbing liquid as they sit, so I always add a little fresh broth to get the consistency right and to wake up the flavor).

4 ounces prosciutto or pancetta, cut into 4 pieces

4 ounces smoked slab bacon, cut into 4 pieces

6 tablespoons extra virgin olive oil plus additional for serving

2 cups diced white onions

Kosher salt and freshly ground black pepper

2 tablespoons minced garlic

1½ tablespoons finely chopped fresh rosemary

1½ tablespoons finely chopped fresh sage

1½ tablespoons tomato paste

2¾ cups Easter Broth (page 8) or chicken broth

3 cups cooked borlotti or other beans, cooking liquid reserved
   (or 1 28-ounce can, rinsed)

1 pound dried short tubular pasta, such as ditalini or elbow macaroni

3 tablespoons unsalted butter

2 tablespoons freshly grated Parmigiano-Reggiano

This recipe is fantastic made with home-cooked beans and homemade broth, but it is still very good pulled together at the last minute with canned beans and broth.

There will be quite a bit of fat in the pot after you render the meat, but don't discard it; you need every bit of it to flavor the beans and broth.

Combine the prosciutto or pancetta, bacon, and oil in a large pot. Cook over medium heat, turning the pieces regularly, until the fat renders. When the meat begins to brown, about 7 minutes, add the onions. Season with salt and pepper and stir to coat the onions with the sizzling fat. Fry the onions, stirring occasionally, until they are soft and begin to color, about 10 minutes more.

Add the garlic and cook, stirring occasionally, until it is soft and fragrant, about 3 minutes. Then add the rosemary and sage.

(recipe continues)

Cook for a minute or two, then stir in the tomato paste. Reduce the heat to medium-low and cook the mixture until it concentrates and darkens, about 5 minutes. Add the broth and half of the beans to the pot and bring to a simmer over medium heat.

Meanwhile, puree the remaining beans in a blender or food processor with just enough of the bean cooking liquid or water to allow the blade to rotate, about ¾ cup (you want the bean puree to be as thick as possible). Scrape the puree into the pot and stir to mix thoroughly. Simmer until the flavors blend, about 10 minutes.

Remove the pieces of cured meat and discard them. Season the bean mixture with salt and pepper and keep warm over low heat. Or you can cool and refrigerate or freeze the beans for later use.

About 10 minutes before you plan to serve, cook the pasta in a large pot of boiling salted water. When it's almost al dente, lift the pasta from the boiling water and add it to the bean mixture. Stir in the butter and Parmigiano. Add a few grinds of pepper and simmer until the pasta is done. Ladle the pasta e fagioli into warm bowls and serve drizzled with oil.

You want to cut the pork into pieces to maximize the surface area of the meat that will be exposed to heat. This increases the amount of flavor you can extract to flavor the beans. But don't cut the pieces too small or they will be hard to retrieve when the time comes.

about making pasta

I use one dough for simple egg pasta like pappardelle (Pasta Dough I), another for stuffed pasta (Pasta Dough II), and a third, a spinach dough, for lasagne (Pasta Dough III). No matter which dough I'm making, the process is the same, and each can be made either completely by hand, using a food processor, or from start to finish in a kitchen mixer with paddle and dough hook attachments.

The most traditional way to make pasta is to mound the flour on a board, make a well in the center, crack the eggs into the well, and add the salt. Using your fingers, you mix the eggs and gradually begin incorporating flour. When the dough comes together, you knead it until it's smooth—about 15 minutes. If you prefer, you can start off in a large mixing bowl, but you'll still need to make a well and get your hands in the dough.

A slightly less time-consuming way to make pasta is to start out in a food processor. Put all of the ingredients in the machine and pulse until the dough resembles pebbles. Then turn the dough out onto a floured board and knead, again for about 15 minutes.

The easiest approach is to use a standing mixer. Put the ingredients in the bowl and, using the paddle attachment, mix until the dough comes together. Switch to the dough hook and knead the dough until it is smooth, about 7 minutes.

Once made, pasta needs to rest. I wrap it in plastic and let it stand at room temperature for 1 hour or refrigerate it overnight. Make sure to allow the dough to come to room temperature before you attempt to roll it—which I do with a machine, either electric or hand-crank. Although some purists swear by hand rolling, I think it's a whole lot of extra work for little or no benefit.

Divide the dough as you go. If you don't, as it stretches it will get so long it's hard to manage. Start at the largest setting and work your way toward the thickness you are looking for. Once the dough is rolled, cut it and put it on a baking sheet dusted with semolina, covering it with a kitchen towel until you're ready to use it. It is best to roll out the dough within a couple of hours of when you plan to use it.

pasta dough I

MAKES 1 POUND

This is the dough to make when you are making fettucine or pappardelle to serve with a hearty sauce like Bolognese (page 22).

2½ cups all-purpose flour
⅓ cup semolina flour
4 eggs
Pinch of salt

For this recipe, you want finely ground semolina. Made from grinding wheat endosperm, semolina flour is higher in gluten than white flour; mixing the two makes pasta more toothsome. Hard wheat semolina is light yellow and looks something like very finely ground corn meal—it's what you want. Whiter soft wheat semolina is usually sold in this country as farina or under the brand name Cream of Wheat and is not a substitute.

Combine the flour, semolina, eggs, and salt in a bowl, a food processor, or a stand mixer with paddle. Work the ingredients together (see "About Making Pasta," page 39) until they are integrated and the dough holds together.

If you use a food processor or are making the dough by hand, turn the dough out onto a clean work surface and knead until it is smooth and no longer sticky, 10 to 15 minutes. If the dough is sticky, add a little more flour. If you use a mixer, switch to the dough hook attachment and knead the dough until it is smooth, about 7 minutes, again adding flour if necessary.

Wrap the dough in plastic wrap and set it aside at room temperature for at least 40 minutes or refrigerate it overnight. Allow the dough to come to room temperature before you roll it out. Roll and cut the dough into the desired shape and cook in boiling salted water until it is just tender.

pasta dough II

MAKES ABOUT ¾ POUND

This is the dough to make for stuffed pasta like tortellini and tortelli.

1¾ cups all-purpose flour
1 egg
4–5 egg yolks
Pinch of salt

Combine the flour, egg, 4 yolks, and salt in a bowl, a food processor, or a stand mixer with a paddle. Work the ingredients together (see "About Making Pasta," page 39) until they are well integrated. If the dough is too dry—you can't form a ball—add the other yolk.

If you use a food processor or are making the dough by hand, turn the dough out onto a clean work surface and knead until it is smooth, 10 to 15 minutes. If the dough is sticky, add a little more flour. If you use a mixer, switch to the dough hook attachment and knead the dough until it is smooth, about 7 minutes, again adding flour if necessary.

Wrap the dough in plastic wrap and set it aside at room temperature for at least 40 minutes or refrigerate it overnight. Allow the dough to come to room temperature before you roll and cut it.

If the dough is still too dry after adding a fifth yolk, you can work in a small amount (less than a tablespoon) of water. And remember the dough will get more elastic as you knead it, so it should be pretty tough when you start.

If you wind up with extra dough after rolling and shaping, cut it into noodles and dry it at room temperature on a baking sheet sprinkled with semolina. Once dried, the pasta will keep indefinitely and can be cooked, then tossed with sauce or butter and cheese.

pasta dough III

MAKES ABOUT 1 POUND

This is a spinach dough, the one to use when you are making Lasagne Verde Bolognese (page 56). Chop the spinach very finely or pulse it in a food processor and remember to squeeze it really dry or the proportions will be off.

¾ cup blanched, drained, very finely chopped spinach
 (about 1¼ pounds raw)

4 eggs

Pinch of salt

3¼ cups all-purpose flour

Combine the spinach, eggs, and salt in a food processor. Pulse the ingredients together (see "About Making Pasta," page 39) until the spinach is finely chopped. Add the flour and pulse until the dough holds together.

Turn the dough out onto a clean work surface and knead until it is smooth, 10 to 15 minutes. If the dough is sticky, add a little more flour.

Wrap the dough in plastic wrap and set it aside at room temperature for 1 hour or refrigerate it overnight. Allow the dough to come to room temperature before you roll it out. Cut the dough into the desired shape and cook it until it is just tender in boiling salted water.

You can use one thawed 10-ounce package of frozen chopped spinach instead of fresh. Roll it in a clean kitchen towel and squeeze it well to remove as much moisture as possible.

I think it is easiest to make this dough in a food processor. Although you can chop the spinach by hand, it is difficult to mince it finely enough.

pappardelle with mushrooms

SERVES 4 TO 6

Good made with one kind of mushroom, this recipe is even better made with a combination. If you can get wild mushrooms, all the better. I also like to include some dried mushrooms, usually porcini (I use the soaking liquid at the end to finish the sauce). Pan-roast each type of mushroom by itself. Cook them over medium-high heat in olive oil and butter, in small batches—the wetter the mushroom, the smaller the batch. You need more hot surface area if the mushrooms are going to give off a lot of moisture so the liquid evaporates on contact. If the mushrooms are dry, you can pretty much fill the pan; but if they aren't, keep the heat high and the pan uncrowded.

How you clean the mushrooms will have an impact on how you cook them. If they are dirty, soak them in several changes of water, and blot them as dry as you can. Then cook them in very small batches.

Pasta Dough I (page 40)

1½ pounds cultivated and wild mushrooms, cleaned
(for more about cooking mushrooms, see page 145)

1 ounce dried porcini mushrooms

¼ cup boiling water

¼ cup extra virgin olive oil

8 tablespoons (1 stick) unsalted butter

Kosher salt and freshly ground black pepper

2 tablespoons finely minced shallot

1 tablespoon minced garlic

2 tablespoons chopped fresh oregano (or thyme, rosemary, or basil)

Pinch of minced peperoncini or red pepper flakes (optional)

1 cup freshly grated Parmigiano-Reggiano

Roll out the pasta dough and cut it into pappardelle, noodles about 5" × 1½".

Trim the fresh mushrooms and cut them into slices, all about the same size. Keep the varieties separate. Place the dried mushrooms in a bowl, add the boiling water, and set aside until they soften, about 15 minutes; strain and reserve the liquid and mushrooms separately.

Heat 1 tablespoon each of oil and butter in a large skillet over high heat. Without mixing the different types, add about a third of the mushrooms (the exact size of each batch will depend on the kind of mushrooms you are cooking). Season with salt and pepper, and cook the mushrooms until they begin to brown, about 3 minutes. Flip them and cook until they are tender and lightly browned, about 3 minutes more. Transfer the mushrooms to a bowl, wipe out the skillet, and repeat the process, adding more butter and oil, then cooking the rest of the mushrooms in batches. Add the soaked porcini to the final batch of mushrooms. (The mushrooms can be pan-roasted several hours in advance.)

Shortly before you wish to eat, bring a large pot of salted water to a boil. Heat 1 tablespoon each of oil and butter in a large skillet over medium heat. Add the shallot and garlic and cook, stirring frequently, until they soften, about 2 minutes. Add the mushrooms and raise the heat to medium-high. Add the oregano and peperoncini if using. Heat the mushrooms through, then add the strained porcini liquid and bring it to a boil.

Add the pappardelle to the boiling water and cook until it floats. Finish cooking the sauce by removing the skillet from the heat and swirling in 4 tablespoons butter, 1 tablespoon at a time.

Lift the pasta out of the water and add it to the mushrooms. Toss the pasta, coating it in the sauce. If the pan seems dry or the pasta is still too chewy, add a few tablespoons of the pasta cooking water. Finish cooking the pasta in the sauce over medium heat just until it is al dente, a minute or two at most. Add half of the Parmigiano, adjust the seasoning with salt and pepper, and serve topped with the remaining Parmigiano.

In Italy, pasta al funghi is flavored with an herb I almost never see here: nepitella, a type of mint that has a hint of oregano in its flavor. If you see it, grab it or consider planting a little.

If you don't use dried porcini, add broth or pasta cooking liquid to the sauce before adding the butter. In order for the emulsification to hold, you must have sufficient liquid in the pan.

pappardelle with duck ragù

SERVES 4

This recipe should be viewed as a blueprint for turning yesterday's braise into a wonderful pasta sauce. Start by frying soffritto (if you have some made already, all the better—if not, it's easy enough to mince a little). You want to get the vegetables a dark caramel color here, then add olives, rosemary, and garlic. Add the braised meat, then wine and broth (or better yet, some of the braising liquid) and simmer until the flavors come together. I use braised duck (see Braised Duck with Niçoise Olives and Rosemary, page 200), but you could use rabbit, beef, pork, lamb, or chicken. You can make this sauce ahead—but it's so quick there's really no need.

This sauce works best with homemade pasta, but you can substitute 1 pound of dried pasta.

If you have Blond Soffritto Base (page 12), start with ¼ cup. Fry it, stirring frequently, until it darkens, about 7 minutes. Then follow the recipe, beginning by bringing the pasta water to a boil.

Pasta Dough I (page 40)

¼ **cup extra virgin olive oil**

½ **cup minced onion**

¼ **cup minced celery**

¼ **cup minced carrot**

Kosher salt and freshly ground black pepper

About 12 pitted niçoise olives

1 fresh rosemary sprig, leaves picked

1 garlic clove, peeled and minced

4 braised duck legs (page 200), skin and bones discarded, meat in large pieces

½ **cup dry red wine**

2 cups strained, reduced duck braising liquid, Easter Broth (page 8), or chicken broth

About ¾ cup freshly grated Parmigiano-Reggiano

6 tablespoons (¾ stick) unsalted butter, cut into 6 pieces

Roll out the pasta dough and cut it into pappardelle, noodles about 5" × 1½".

Heat the oil in a large high-sided skillet over medium-high heat. Add the onion, celery, and carrot and fry; the soffritto should sizzle as it cooks. Stir occasionally at first, then more frequently as the mixture begins to color and reduce in volume. Continue frying, stirring often to prevent scorching, until the soffritto has reduced by half and is a rich brown, about 15 minutes.

While the soffritto cooks, bring a large pot of salted water to a boil.

Shortly before you drop the pasta into the water, add the olives, rosemary, and garlic to the soffritto. Fry, stirring to mix, until the garlic is fragrant, about 2 minutes. Add the duck and mix gently to coat the meat with soffritto and olives. Add the wine to the pan—it will evaporate quickly. Add the braising liquid or broth and simmer vigorously, reducing until the sauce is slightly viscous (the sauce will thin when the pasta is added).

You want the pieces of duck to stay a good size, so don't stir the sauce so much that they shred.

Add the pasta to the boiling water and cook until the noodles float.

Stir ½ cup Parmigiano and 4 tablespoons butter into the sauce. Lift the pasta from the water and add it to the sauce (along with a little of the pasta cooking water if the sauce seems tight). Let the pasta simmer until it is al dente, about 2 minutes.

Season the pasta and sauce with salt and pepper and toss gently. Add the remaining 2 tablespoons butter, then divide the pasta among warm bowls. Serve topped with the remaining Parmigiano and a bit more fresh pepper.

pumpkin tortelli

SERVES 4 TO 6

Experts believe tortelli recipes found in old Florentine cookbooks are the earliest form of stuffed pasta made in Italy. Similar to ravioli, tortelli are round, square, or as here triangular pasta "sandwiches." This savory squash filling with a hint of sweetness is very typical. I add mostarda, a traditional fruit preserve spiced with mustard oil, and I add crumbled amaretti cookies. You can omit either or both, but I just don't think the tortelli are anywhere near as good. Both are sold at specialty stores and available by mail.

FOR THE TORTELLI:

Winter squash yields vary considerably, so I always err on the side of roasting too much rather than too little. Extra filling freezes beautifully. For more about batch size, see page 51.

2 pounds orange winter squash, such as butternut, kabocha, or cheese pumpkin (the true "zucca" found throughout Italy), halved

4 tablespoons (½ stick) unsalted butter

2 teaspoons chopped fresh sage

Kosher salt and freshly ground black pepper

½ white onion, peeled and finely chopped

⅓ cup freshly grated Parmigiano-Reggiano

4 ounces imported Italian amaretti cookies, crumbled

½ cup chopped mostarda fruit

Pinch of freshly grated nutmeg

Pasta Dough II (page 41)

FOR THE SAUCE:

½ pound (2 sticks) unsalted butter

1 tablespoon finely chopped fresh sage

Kosher salt and freshly ground black pepper

¼ cup freshly grated Parmigiano-Reggiano

Here, as whenever you prepare stuffed pasta, make sure the filling is as dry as it can be. I roast the squash a day ahead and let it drain in the refrigerator overnight.

TO MAKE THE TORTELLI: Preheat the oven to 350°F. Place the squash halves on a baking sheet, cut side up. Put 1 tablespoon butter in each, then season with sage, salt, and pepper. Cover with aluminum foil and bake the squash until soft, about 2 hours.

Spoon the squash out of their skins and transfer to a food processor. Pulse until the puree is smooth. Wrap the puree in cheesecloth, then place in a strainer set over a bowl in the refrigerator. Allow the pureed squash to drain overnight.

The next day, melt 2 tablespoons butter in a medium skillet over medium-low heat. Add the onion and sweat (cook without coloring), stirring occasionally, about 10 minutes. Transfer the onion to a mixing bowl.

Add the squash puree, Parmigiano, cookies, and fruit to the bowl and mix to combine. Season the filling well with salt, pepper, and nutmeg.

Divide the dough into quarters. Stretch each piece and thin it using a pasta machine, working from the largest setting to the smallest. Lay the pasta sheets on a lightly floured work surface.

To form the tortelli, use a ravioli cutter or knife to cut out 3" squares. Put a heaping teaspoonful of the filling in the center of each square. Fold the pasta over the filling, bringing one corner to meet its diagonal opposite. Press the pasta together, crimping to make a seal, then bring both corners of the base of the triangle together to form a little hat, crimping and sealing. Place the finished tortelli on a floured baking sheet. When you're done, cover the tortelli with a clean dish towel if they are going to stand for more than 30 minutes.

Bring a large pot of salted water to a boil. Add the tortelli and cook until they float to the surface and are fully tender, about 5 minutes.

TO MAKE THE SAUCE: While the tortelli cook, melt the butter in a large skillet over medium-low heat. Allow it to cook until it is nut brown. Add the sage. Lift the tortelli out of the cooking water and into the skillet with a slotted spoon. Season with salt and pepper, toss the pasta in the browned butter, and serve topped with Parmigiano.

tortellini in broth

SERVES 6

Making the filling for tortellini in a food processor is much easier than mincing everything by hand, but you need to make enough to allow the machine to function properly—which means making more than you'll need for this recipe. That's okay; just make the whole batch, freeze them on baking sheets, then transfer them to freezer bags to use in the future in broth or with ragù or simply with butter and cheese.

1 boneless, skinless chicken breast (about 5 ounces)

1 piece prosciutto (1½ ounces)

1 piece mortadella (1½ ounces)

1 tablespoon unsalted butter

1 tablespoon extra virgin olive oil

1 small garlic clove, peeled and thinly sliced

Kosher salt and freshly ground black pepper

1 egg yolk

⅓ cup freshly grated Parmigiano-Reggiano
   plus additional for serving

Pinch of freshly grated nutmeg

½ recipe Pasta Dough II (page 41)

10 cups Easter Broth (page 8) or chicken broth

Dice the chicken, prosciutto, and mortadella (you don't have to be too finicky—the meat is going into the food processor after it's cooked).

Combine the butter and oil in a large skillet over high heat. Add the garlic and the meat mixture; season with salt and pepper. Reduce the heat to medium and cook, stirring frequently, until the chicken is cooked through, about 5 minutes.

Transfer the meat mixture to a food processor. Pulse the machine once or twice, then add the egg yolk, Parmigiano, and nutmeg. Season the filling with pepper and pulse the processor until the filling is minced and mixed.

Divide the dough into quarters. Stretch each piece and thin it using a pasta machine, working from the largest setting to the smallest. Flour your table or board and lay out the rolled dough. Cut the dough into circles, each about 2" across. (If you don't have a cutter, a wine glass will work.) Put about ½ teaspoon filling in the center of each circle. Fold each piece in half. Press down firmly to secure the edges. You will now have semicircles. Pick each up, holding the straight base parallel to the table, then bring the two corners together. Press tightly. Place the tortellini on a clean towel, discard the scraps of pasta dough, and repeat the process with the remaining dough.

Heat the broth in a large pot over high heat. Season with salt and pepper. When the broth boils, add the tortellini, a few at a time, until you've added 60 (10 per person). Allow the broth to return to a boil, then reduce the heat to a simmer and cook the tortellini until they float, about 4 minutes. Ladle the tortellini and broth into six bowls. Serve sprinkled with Parmigiano.

For a heartier soup, substitute tortellini, 4 to 6 per serving, for the dumplings and farro in the recipe for Chicken Soup with Escarole, Farro, and Dumplings (page 84).

batch size

One thing that distinguishes chefs from good home cooks is the way we use batch size to our advantage in the kitchen. Tortellini filling is a perfect example. It's quicker and easier to use the food processor to make it, but I can use the machine only if I make more than I need. My mother would likely get out the knife—and that's fine, just less efficient. I, on the other hand, go ahead and make more than I need because I know the formed tortellini will come in handy later. And if I don't have time to make them all, I know the filling can be frozen until I do. With the tortellini filling, it's the machine that suggests my approach; other times, I simply increase the batch because it is as easy to do so as not. I do this with lots of things: Soffritto and broth are obvious examples but hardly unique. I might wash enough lettuce for 2 days rather than one (it will keep wrapped in paper towels in a sealed plastic bag) or braise more short ribs than I want—I can serve them as is or use the meat in a pasta filling or sauce (see Pappardelle with Duck Ragù, page 46). Believe me, this approach is just as effective at home as it is in a restaurant. Just be aware of the shelf life of the prepared food and your storage capacity.

cannelloni with spinach and ricotta

SERVES 4 TO 6

The key to this recipe and the next one is getting the spinach really dry. Squeeze the blanched spinach in a dish towel, not all at once but in small batches. Squeeze until you think you can't get any more liquid out, then squeeze it a little more for good measure. Let the ricotta drain overnight.

The same filling can be used to make ravioli.

2 pounds fresh ricotta cheese

1¼ cups cooked spinach (about 12 ounces raw)

1½ cups freshly grated Parmigiano-Reggiano plus additional for garnish

2 tablespoons extra virgin olive oil

Kosher salt and freshly ground black pepper

Pinch of freshly grated nutmeg

Pasta Dough II (page 41)

Tuscan Tomato Sauce (page 19) or Rich Tomato Sauce (page 20)

You have enough filling to make about 20 cannelloni, depending on how generously you fill them. I serve two or three per person for an appetizer and four as an entrée. If the numbers don't work perfectly (and they probably won't), freeze any leftover filled cannelloni. Then reheat in a 350°F oven, covered with sauce and foil.

Wrap the ricotta in cheesecloth and put it in a sieve set over a bowl. Put something heavy on top, then allow the ricotta to drain overnight in the refrigerator.

Squeeze the spinach as dry as possible, then mince it (you can do this in a food processor—just be sure to pulse and stop short of pureeing the spinach; you want some texture). Combine the spinach, ricotta, Parmigiano, and oil in a bowl. Season generously with salt, pepper, and nutmeg and mix well.

Preheat the oven to 350°F. Bring a large pot of salted water to a boil. Fill a large bowl with ice water.

Divide the dough in half. Stretch each piece and thin it using a pasta machine, working from the largest setting to the smallest. Lay the pasta sheets on a lightly floured work surface and cut each into about ten 5" × 3" rectangles. Cook the pasta in the boiling water, a few pieces at a time, just until they float, about 2 minutes. Cool the pasta sheets by dropping them into the ice water. Drain them, then lay the pieces in single layers on clean dish towels.

Form the cannelloni: Spoon a few tablespoons of filling onto each pasta rectangle, then roll into a cylinder (you want to wind up with between 16 and 20). Spoon a layer of tomato sauce onto the bottom of a baking dish large enough to hold the cannelloni in a single snug layer. Arrange the cannelloni in the dish, spoon more sauce on top, then sprinkle generously with Parmigiano. Bake the cannelloni, uncovered, until the sauce is bubbly and the pasta is beginning to color, about 20 minutes. Rest the cannelloni for 5 to 10 minutes, then serve.

If you wind up with some extra pasta dough, roll it and cut it into pappardelle or fettuccine, then dry it and keep it in a bag in the freezer to use later.

swiss chard and parmigiano malfatti

SERVES 6

Malfatti (literally "badly formed"), also known as ravioli nudi (naked ravioli), are tender dumplings of cheese and chard "filling" that can be served topped with tomato sauce, melted butter and cheese, or, as here, finished in a little broth. The trick to malfatti is making sure to eliminate as much liquid as possible. If there is extra moisture, the malfatti will not hold together. It works best to start a day ahead. Blanch, chop, and squeeze the chard, then put it in a strainer, weight it, and let it drain overnight. Also weight and drain the ricotta overnight.

Malfatti can be made with virtually any leafy green. Spinach and chard are most common. I prefer chard because I like the flavor and it contains less water than spinach.

3 pounds Swiss chard

2 cups fresh ricotta cheese

1½ cups freshly grated Parmigiano-Reggiano
    plus additional for serving

3 egg yolks

Kosher salt and freshly ground black pepper

Pinch of freshly grated nutmeg

About ½ cup all-purpose flour

6 cups Easter Broth (page 8) or chicken broth

Chard stems are very good blanched, then warmed in butter or olive oil and served as a side dish with roasted meat. Or put the blanched chard stems in a baking dish and top them with a layer of bread crumbs and some freshly grated Parmigiano. Dot the top with butter and brown under the broiler for about 5 minutes.

Separate the chard leaves from the stems. Reserve the stems for another use. Blanch the chard leaves in a large pot of boiling salted water until they are tender, about 3 minutes. Drain the chard and plunge immediately into ice water to cool and set the color. Drain the chard well, then chop finely (or pulse it in a food processor). Squeeze the chard dry in a kitchen towel in small batches, getting it as dry as possible. Wrap the chard in a kitchen towel, place it in a strainer set over a bowl, then add weight (a large can of tomatoes is good). Refrigerate the chard and allow it to drain overnight.

Wrap the ricotta in cheesecloth; put it in a strainer set over a bowl. Weight the cheese and refrigerate it, allowing it to drain overnight.

Combine the drained chard and ricotta in a mixing bowl (discarding any liquids that have accumulated). Add the Parmigiano and egg yolks and season with salt, pepper, and nutmeg. Mix vigorously to distribute the chard.

Bring a large pot of salted water to a boil. Lightly flour your hands and form the ricotta mixture into small balls.

Working in batches, cook the malfatti in the boiling water. They are done when they float to the surface, about 3 minutes. Using a slotted spoon, remove the malfatti from the water and arrange them in warm bowls (keep the bowls at the back of the stove so the cooked malfatti don't cool while you cook subsequent batches).

While the malfatti cooks, heat the broth in a saucepan over medium-high heat. Season to taste with salt and pepper. Divide the broth among the bowls, top each portion with Parmigiano, and serve.

lasagne verde bolognese

SERVES 6

This is a very traditional lasagne: many layers of homemade pasta, creamy béchamel, and meaty Bolognese sauce. I serve it at Insieme, where it's probably the most popular dish on the menu. (I am forever grateful to Ruth Reichl, editor in chief of Gourmet, *who declared it the best lasagne in New York City.) It's important to roll the pasta out thinly; if it's too thick, the lasagne will lack the delicacy and balance you're looking for. It's a lot of work, which you just can't rush. But if you stretch it out over a couple of days, making the sauce and pasta one day, then assembling and baking the lasagne the next, it's not too bad—and the end result is really, really delicious.*

FOR THE BÉCHAMEL:

> 6 tablespoons (¾ stick) unsalted butter
>
> 4½ tablespoons all-purpose flour
>
> 3 cups whole milk
>
> Kosher salt and freshly ground black pepper
>
> Pinch of freshly grated nutmeg

FOR THE LASAGNE:

> ½ recipe Pasta Dough III (page 42)
>
> Bolognese Sauce (page 22)
>
> 2¼ cups freshly grated Parmigiano-Reggiano

Do not substitute commercial lasagne noodles for homemade pasta in this recipe. They will be too thick.

TO MAKE THE BÉCHAMEL: Melt the butter in a high-sided, heavy-bottomed saucepan. Whisk in the flour and then the milk. Bring to a boil, whisking constantly. (Watch the pan, because the milk has a tendency to boil over.) When the sauce reaches a boil, adjust the heat so it is actively simmering. Cook, stirring frequently, first with a whisk and then with a wooden spoon, until the sauce thickens, about 25 minutes. Season the béchamel with salt, pepper, and nutmeg and keep warm over very low heat.

TO MAKE THE LASAGNE: Divide the dough into thirds. Stretch each piece and thin it using a pasta machine, working from the largest to the smallest setting but stopping just short of the last setting. Once a portion of dough has been stretched, cut it into sheets the length of the baking dish you plan to use (an 11" × 9" pan works well). Lay the lasagne sheets on a baking

(recipe continues)

sheet sprinkled with flour. Cover each layer with plastic wrap and sprinkle the plastic with more flour. Cover the top layer with a kitchen towel.

Shortly before you are ready to assemble the lasagne, bring a large pot of salted water to a boil and fill a large bowl with ice water. Quickly cook the pasta sheets, a few at a time, in the boiling water, retrieving them when they float. Immediately drop them into the ice water to stop the cooking. Once they are cool, take the pasta out of the ice water and arrange them in a single layer on clean dish towels until you are ready to use them. (When I was growing up, we always covered the kitchen table with a sheet.)

TO ASSEMBLE THE LASAGNE: Spoon just enough Bolognese sauce into the baking dish to moisten the bottom. Strain the béchamel through a fine sieve, then spoon a thin layer over the Bolognese sauce. Sprinkle the first layer evenly with Parmigiano. Place pasta sheets on top, covering the sauce and cheese without overlapping (two should do it, but don't hesitate to cut the pasta to fit your pan). Build about 8 more layers in the same fashion and end with a generous topping of Bolognese, béchamel, and Parmigiano. (The lasagne can be assembled and refrigerated up to a day in advance.)

Preheat the oven to 350°F. Bake the lasagne until it is bubbly, about 35 minutes. Remove from the oven and let it rest for at least 20 minutes before serving.

gnocchi

SERVES 4 TO 6

In my experience, recipes with the fewest elements are often the most difficult to master. A variation in one ingredient can have a huge effect on the finished product. In this case, it's the potato that tends to create problems. Potatoes vary in size, which means baking times will differ. Starch levels range, which controls how much you'll need to "work" the dough. And moisture contents are not the same, which affects how much flour is required. Even though I've tried to be as specific as I can about quantities and passed along all my tips and advice on the process of making this dough, the truth is the way to get good at making gnocchi is by doing it again and again—really paying attention to what you're seeing and feeling as you go.

3 large russet (Idaho) potatoes, scrubbed

Freshly ground white pepper

1 egg yolk

About 2⅓ cups all-purpose flour

About 4 tablespoons (½ stick) unsalted butter, diced

1 tablespoon chopped fresh sage

Kosher salt and freshly ground black pepper

About ¼ cup freshly grated Parmigiano-Reggiano

Although some people use Yukon Gold potatoes to make gnocchi, I find starchy Idaho produce a lighter result.

Heat the oven to 350°F. Prick the potatoes with a fork and bake them until they are soft, about 1½ hours.

While they're still hot, cut all of the potatoes in half lengthwise—you want to create as much surface area as possible so the steam billows out. (Steam is water; the less water the potatoes contain, the less flour you will need. The less flour, the lighter your gnocchi.) Scoop the potatoes out of the skins and into a fine-holed ricer. Pass them through the ricer onto a large clean work surface—use your countertop or kitchen table. Using the end of a large metal kitchen spoon, spread the potatoes into an even rectangle about 24" × 12".

Season the potatoes generously with white pepper. When they are no longer hot to the touch, almost room temperature, beat the egg yolk. Drizzle the yolk over the potatoes. Measure 1¼ cups flour and sprinkle this over the potatoes.

Gnocchi are very good topped with tomato sauce. Try the Amatriciana Sauce (page 21) or the Bolognese Sauce (page 22) or consider the duck ragù (see Pappardelle with Duck Ragù, page 46).

(recipe continues)

Using a pastry scraper, cut the flour and egg into the potatoes, chopping and then turning the mixture in on itself and folding it together, until everything is well mixed and the dough resembles coarse crumbs. Bring the mixture together into a ball.

Sprinkle a scant ¼ cup flour on the work surface. Place the dough on the flour and press down, flattening it into a disk with both hands. Dust the dough with another scant ¾ cup flour. Using your hands, fold and press the dough until the flour is incorporated. Add two dustings of flour to the work surface and dough and repeat. If the dough still feels tacky, repeat once more, this time covering both the table and the dough with no more than 2 tablespoons flour.

Roll the dough into a compact log. Dust the outside with flour, then allow the dough to rest for about 5 minutes. Dust the work surface lightly with flour. Divide the log into 8 pieces. Roll each section into a cylinder about ½" thick. Using a floured knife or pastry cutter, cut the dough into gnocchi about 1" long.

I cut gnocchi smaller or larger depending upon how I plan to serve them.

Bring a pot of heavily salted water to a boil. Working in two or three batches, drop the gnocchi into the water and cook, stirring occasionally, until they float, 2 to 3 minutes. Retrieve the gnocchi with a slotted spoon and put them on a baking sheet or plate.

While the gnocchi cook, melt the butter in a large skillet over medium heat. Add the sage and season with salt and black pepper. Allow the butter to brown slightly, about 4 minutes. Add the gnocchi to the browned butter and remove the pan from the heat. Mix gently and serve topped with Parmigiano.

about risotto

Risotto is no more than rice cooked in broth flavored with some onion. Add a little butter and Parmesan cheese and you have it. It's a litmus test for a professional kitchen. If the risotto is good, there's somebody back there with finesse, paying attention; that's what it takes—it's not hard, but it requires a little skill and awareness. The happy truth is it's easier at home. You can focus, follow a few simple rules, and learn to "feel" the rice as it moves from raw to perfectly cooked. Start to finish, it takes around 20 minutes, an eternity in a restaurant kitchen but a wholly reasonable amount of time to devote to making a delicious dish at home.

The process is straightforward.

1. Sweat onions over low heat in a mixture of butter and olive oil.

2. Turn up the heat and add the rice. Cook, stirring to coat the rice with fat and onion, until the rice starts to crackle, a sign it is getting hot.

3. Add wine (most often but not always white) and allow it to bubble vigorously; stir frequently, until the rice absorbs the wine—this will take under a minute.

4. Start gradually adding warm broth, enough to just cover the rice. Simmer, stirring occasionally, until the pan is nearly dry. Then cover the rice with broth again.

5. After the second addition of broth, once the rice starts to soften, add broth in smaller increments, about ¼ cup. Now you need to stir more or less constantly, add broth a little at a time, and taste the rice often.

6. When the rice is just tender but still holding its shape, the grains bound loosely by the now creamy broth, pull the pot off the stove and add butter and cheese to finish the risotto; adjust the seasoning.

So what's the secret? There are several. Start by picking the right pan. You want one with a good thick bottom that has straight sides at least 2 inches high and a good amount of surface area. I use a rondeau. You can also use a straight-sided skillet or a saucepan with a lot of surface area.

The cooking process begins with sweating the onions then sautéing the rice in flavorful hot fat. Turn the heat up. The rice should get hot enough to "crackle and pop" and really start to cook in the fat, not merely bathe in it. Once you start adding liquid, you want the liquid in the pan to be boiling all the time. This means you should work over medium-high heat, particularly at the beginning, when you are adding generous amounts of liquid. As you decrease the amount of liquid you're adding, I find that the same simmer can be maintained over less intense heat, so be sure to adjust as the rice cooks.

The exact amount of broth you'll need to add will depend on a lot of factors, including the kind of rice (pick a variety grown in northern Italy, like Arborio, Carnaroli, or Vialone), what other ingredients you have included, and how chewy you like your rice and how dry you like your risotto—ultimately matters of personal taste. Remember that the rice will continue to absorb moisture even after it's removed from the heat. I stop cooking when the risotto seems a little runny, work in butter and Parmigiano-Reggiano, and season with salt and pepper off the heat. Then by the time it gets to the table, it's just right.

Stirring risotto is essential, but it's not necessary to do it constantly throughout. I start off stirring just enough to keep the rice from sticking. When the rice is covered with broth, it cooks evenly without much attention. Later on, when you're adding less broth, stir more often. At the end, stir constantly; this keeps the rice cooking evenly.

The very best risotto is made without interruption of the cooking process. So when you can, make the time and do it right. But I'd be holding back if I didn't tell you it's possible to cheat and still get very good results. Many restaurants get a jump on things several hours before service, cooking risotto halfway (through the absorption of the second addition of liquid, step 4, page 63) and then cooling it quickly by spreading it on baking sheets. The risotto is then revived and finished to order by adding additional broth. This method, while not perfect, works, and it's useful to know about. The final cooking goes quickly, just 5 minutes or so, manageable even when you're entertaining.

Once you understand the basic method, you can begin to play with flavored risotto. The possibilities are nearly endless. On the following pages, you will find recipes for Corn and Pancetta Risotto (page 66) and Asparagus Risotto (page 68); also see Porcini Risotto Balls (page 70). These recipes should give you a feel for the process. I've also included a few ideas below that you might consider. Just keep in mind as you develop your own combinations that you want to add ingredients at the point where they flavor the rice without over- or undercooking them.

more risotto ideas

In each case, start with 2 cups of Arborio or other short-grained rice. Expect to add 1 cup of wine and 6 to 8 cups of broth, making enough risotto to serve six to eight as a first course.

LEMON AND HERB RISOTTO Proceed as described but mix in ½ cup finely chopped fresh herbs (basil, flat-leaf parsley, chervil, or tarragon by itself or with a little dill or mint) when you add the last ¼ cup broth. Season the risotto with freshly squeezed lemon juice when you add the butter and Parmigiano.

SWEET SAUSAGE AND BLACK CABBAGE (CAVOLO NERO) RISOTTO Brown ¼ pound Italian sausage (removed from the casing) in the pan you will use to cook the risotto. Reserve the sausage. Use the fat to sweat the onion. Proceed as described, adding the diced sausage and 2 cups thinly slivered black cabbage halfway through the first addition of broth.

CALAMARI AND SAFFRON RISOTTO Sauté the rice and add the wine as described. Add a pinch of crumbled saffron to a cup of hot broth before you make the third addition. Continue as described, adding ½ pound very thinly sliced calamari with the last ¼ cup broth. Season with a squeeze of lemon juice at the table.

DUCK AND BAROLO RISOTTO Sauté the rice as described. Add Barolo (or more economically, another hearty red wine) in step 3. Proceed as described, adding 2 cups chopped braised duck (see Braised Duck with Niçoise Olives and Rosemary, page 200) when you begin adding broth in ¼-cup increments.

SWEET PEA RISOTTO Render ¼ pound finely diced prosciutto with the butter and oil. Remove the prosciutto and reserve. Sweat the onions and proceed as described, adding 2 cups fresh shelled peas when you begin adding broth in ¼-cup increments. Stir in 1 cup fresh pea shoots and the rendered prosciutto just before removing the risotto from the heat.

corn and pancetta risotto

SERVES 6 TO 8

Corn and pancetta risotto can be made a number of ways, all equally good. The corn can be precooked—grilled or sweated in butter—then added with the last ladle of broth. Or if it's fresh, young, and tender, you can add raw corn a bit earlier in the process.

If you like, you can render the pancetta in your pot, then add the onion and rice to start the risotto. Made this way, the dish will have a more assertively meaty flavor—perfect with grilled corn.

¼ pound thinly sliced pancetta

4 ears of corn, husked

6–8 cups Easter Broth (page 8) or chicken broth

Kosher salt and freshly ground black pepper

4 tablespoons (½ stick) unsalted butter

About 2 tablespoons extra virgin olive oil

1 large onion, peeled and diced

2 cups Arborio or other short-grained rice

¾ cup dry white wine

½ cup freshly grated Parmigiano-Reggiano

Preheat the oven to 400°F. Divide the pancetta between 2 rimmed baking sheets, laying it out in a single layer. Bake the pancetta until the fat renders and the meat is beginning to crisp, 7 to 10 minutes. Pour off the rendered fat and reserve it. Chop the pancetta; add the chopped pancetta to the fat and set the mixture aside.

While the pancetta cooks, cut the corn from the cobs. Reserve the corn kernels; break the cobs in half and put them in a large pot. Add the broth and bring to a simmer over high heat. Reduce the heat slightly and simmer until the broth has reduced by one-third, about 30 minutes. Remove and discard the cobs. Season the broth lightly with salt and pepper and reserve.

Melt 2 tablespoons butter in a rondeau or high-sided skillet over medium heat. Add enough oil so the bottom of the pan is generously coated, about 2 tablespoons. Add the onion, season with salt and pepper, and cook, stirring occasionally, until it softens, about 10 minutes.

Increase the heat to high and add the rice. Using a wooden spoon, stir the rice with the onion and fat until the rice no longer looks chalky and the grains begin to crackle, 2 to 3 minutes.

Make sure the pan is really hot, then add the wine. The wine will almost immediately begin to boil. Stir constantly until the rice absorbs the wine, about 1 minute.

Add enough warm broth to just cover the rice, 1½ to 2 cups. Cook at an active simmer, stirring and scraping the rice away from the sides occasionally. As the rice cooks, the broth will become viscous. Cook the rice until it is once again almost dry, about 5 minutes. Then again add enough broth to cover. Add the raw corn and simmer, scraping and stirring every so often, until the broth is incorporated, about 5 minutes more. (The risotto can be made several hours ahead up to this point. Simply spread the hot rice on a baking sheet and cool. Cover and refrigerate until ready to reheat and complete the recipe.)

At this point, add the pancetta and fat and no more than ½ cup broth. Stir frequently and add broth in small increments until the rice is just tender. Depending upon the age of the rice and how soft and brothy you like your risotto, you can expect to add 1 to 2 cups more in all. Just take care to go slowly so you don't add too much.

Stir in the Parmigiano and the remaining 2 tablespoons butter. Taste and adjust the seasoning with salt and pepper and serve.

Try adding chopped fresh herbs when you add the butter. I think basil goes particularly well with corn.

asparagus risotto

SERVES 6 TO 8

I use slim young asparagus and slice them thinly when I make this. I want the asparagus to cook quickly and maintain its bright green color. If you have larger asparagus, cut them in half lengthwise first, then slice them.

5 tablespoons unsalted butter

2 tablespoons extra virgin olive oil

1 large onion, peeled and diced

Kosher salt and freshly ground black pepper

2 cups Arborio or other short-grained rice

1 cup dry white wine

6–8 cups Easter Broth (page 8) or chicken broth

1 pound asparagus, trimmed and sliced

1 cup freshly grated Parmigiano-Reggiano

You can substitute sliced grilled asparagus for the raw. Add it when you add the butter and cheese.

Heat 2 tablespoons butter and the oil in a large high-sided skillet or rondeau over medium heat. Add the onion, season with salt and pepper, and cook, stirring occasionally, until it begins to soften, about 5 minutes.

Raise the heat to high and add the rice. Using a wooden spoon, stir the rice with the onion and fat until the rice no longer looks chalky and the grains begin to pop, 2 to 3 minutes. Add the wine. Allow it to bubble vigorously until the rice absorbs it, about 1 minute.

Add enough broth to just cover the rice, about 2 cups. Simmer, stirring and scraping rice away from the sides occasionally. Cook the rice until it is almost dry, about 5 minutes, then again add enough broth to cover. Simmer, scraping and stirring every so often, until the broth is incorporated, about 5 minutes more.

Add about 1 cup broth. Stirring more frequently now, cook the risotto until the rice absorbs the broth, about 3 minutes. Add a little more broth. Simmer, stirring, until the pan is almost dry again, about 3 minutes more.

For a more dramatic presentation, stir ½ cup asparagus puree (see Chilled Asparagus Soup with Ramps on page 81) into the risotto when you add the butter and cheese at the end. At the restaurant, we top each portion with a raw quail egg.

Lower the heat and add the asparagus, salt, pepper, and about ¼ cup broth. Simmer, stirring constantly and adding broth in ¼-cup increments, until the rice is just tender. Take the pan off the heat and add the Parmigiano and the remaining 3 tablespoons butter. Taste and adjust the seasoning with salt and pepper, then serve.

porcini risotto balls (arancini)

MAKES ABOUT 30

Reconstitute dried porcinis in warm water and you have mushrooms that taste amazing, deep, and earthy; a richly flavorful broth; and the beginnings of a classic risotto con funghi. Stop there or take it a step further and make arancini—a great hors d'oeuvre. Fry the risotto balls and serve them hot. If you want to get fancy, try stuffing each one with a cube of fontina or mozzarella.

You can serve the risotto on its own. Stir in an additional 3 tablespoons of butter just before serving and sprinkle with additional grated Parmesan cheese to taste. This recipe will serve 4.

FOR THE RISOTTO:

About 5 cups Easter Broth (page 8) or chicken broth

½ cup dried porcini mushrooms

1 tablespoon extra virgin olive oil

1 tablespoon unsalted butter

1 small yellow onion, peeled and diced

1½ cups Arborio rice

½ cup dry white wine

Kosher salt and freshly ground black pepper

½ cup freshly grated Parmigiano-Reggiano

FOR THE ARANCINI:

¾ cup all-purpose flour

2 eggs, beaten

¾ cup fine bread crumbs

Oil for frying

TO MAKE THE RISOTTO: Bring 1 cup broth to a simmer in a saucepan over medium-high heat. Add the mushrooms. Remove the pan from the heat and set the mushrooms aside until they soften, about 20 minutes. Drain the mushrooms, reserving the mushroom-flavored broth. Strain the broth through a fine strainer. Finely chop the mushrooms. Add the chopped mushrooms to the mushroom broth.

Bring the remaining broth to a simmer in a saucepan and keep warm over low heat.

Combine the oil and butter in a large high-sided skillet. Heat over medium heat until the butter foams. Add the onion and cook until it is soft, about 15 minutes. Raise the heat and stir in the rice, thoroughly coating it with the onion, butter, and oil. Cook the rice until you hear it crackle, about 5 minutes. Add the wine and simmer, stirring frequently, until the pan is almost dry.

Add 1 cup broth. Simmer, stirring frequently, until the rice is almost dry. Repeat twice more. Stir the reserved porcini and their broth into the rice; cook, stirring frequently, until the pan looks dry again.

Keep cooking the rice by stirring in enough additional warm broth, a little at a time. Cook the rice until it is soft but still holding its shape. Season with salt and pepper and stir in the Parmigiano-Reggiano. Spread the risotto on a baking sheet and allow it to cool to room temperature.

When making arancini, you want to overcook the rice a little bit. This helps to generate more starch and allows you to form rice balls that will hold together better than if you tried to make them with al dente rice.

TO MAKE ARANCINI: Get your hands a little wet to keep them from getting sticky, then form balls from the rice (we make them about the size of golf balls). Set up a breading station, putting the flour, beaten eggs, and bread crumbs in three separate bowls. Roll the arancini in flour, dip in egg, and roll in bread crumbs to coat.

Heat about ¼" oil in a large high-sided skillet over medium-high heat. When the oil reaches about 360°F (a drop of water will sizzle and sputter when it hits the oil), fry the arancini in small batches, turning them to brown on all sides, about 6 minutes in all. Drain on paper towels, sprinkle with salt, and serve warm.

soups

Italian cooking has a rich tradition of soup making. As with pasta, the recipes run from hearty country fare to very refined dishes. In this chapter, I've included simple rustic soups and soups that work as the main event in an informal supper, as well as refined soups perfectly appropriate to an elegant multicourse meal. In addition to these well-loved traditional recipes, I've included some soups that have a more modern heritage—recipes that have the same kind of flavor integrity as traditional Italian cooking and that I just couldn't omit. Several of my pureed soups fall into this category.

Vegetable purees are about purity—capturing the essence of the vegetable you're working with and adding as little else as possible. The Parsnip Soup recipe (page 77) is a perfect example. Simmer parsnips in seasoned water until soft, then puree them with the cooking liquid. Add a little water and you have a puree, a bit more and you have a soup. No stock, no herbs, just pure vegetable flavor. This method works well with many sweet fall and winter vegetables—cauliflower, celery root, and winter squash all are delicious. It also works well with bright green spring vegetables like peas and asparagus, but because you want to make sure to lock in the color, you have to be extra careful (see the notes for Sweet Pea Soup, page 76, and Chilled Asparagus Soup with Ramps, page 81).

Once the puree is made, I always pass it through a fine sieve. Could you skip this step? Sure, but I find it gives the puree a silky texture that is pretty sexy. You need a really fine sieve, and you need to work the puree through by pressing with a ladle. This is tedious, but it makes a big difference. Another thing you might consider is blending in some kind of fat to add flavor and richness. Butter, olive oil, and crème fraîche all work well.

So what vegetables don't make good purees? I stay away from anything too bitter or strongly flavored, like escarole or cabbage. And some vegetables, like peppers (see Yellow Pepper Soup, page 78), are best cooked with soffritto and beg for a little potato to thicken the puree.

Pureed soups freeze beautifully. If you're tight on space, when you're cooking add just enough water to loosen the puree. This way, it can be stored in small portions (maybe in an ice cube tray; once frozen, transfer the cubes to a plastic bag) and reconstituted later with a little extra water.

sweet pea soup

SERVES 4

At the restaurant, my stove is so powerful I can boil the peas and sweated onions together and get them hot enough that the peas don't pale and dull the color of my soup. At home, my stove just doesn't get the job done, so I blanch the peas first. The extra step is worth it. I like to serve this soup chilled with a little crab and slivered mint. The soup is quite good made with frozen peas, and you don't even need to blanch them.

You'll need about 3½ pounds of peas in their pods to yield 4 cups.

4 cups shelled peas

3 tablespoons unsalted butter

2 cups diced onions

4 cups boiling water

Kosher salt and freshly ground black pepper

Shocking the peas in an ice-water bath after they're blanched and again after they're cooked with the onions is essential to keeping their bright color. Get a big pot and fill it with ice and water—empty your ice trays. Put the peas and onions in a metal bowl and then rest the bowl on the ice water; stir the peas and onions (and their cooking liquid) until everything is cool.

Bring a large pot of salted water to a boil. Fill a large bowl with ice and water. Blanch the peas by dropping them into the boiling water and leaving them until they are bright green (the time will vary depending upon the size and age of the peas).

Drain the peas in a sieve, then **cool them by submerging the sieve in the ice water.** Remove the peas from the water and reserve them.

Melt the butter in a large deep skillet over medium-low heat. Add the onions, season with salt and pepper, cover, and sweat them (cook in their own juices until they are soft but not yet beginning to color), about 7 minutes.

Add the drained peas and stir to coat with the butter and onions. Season with salt and pepper and add the boiling water. Cook the peas over high heat until they are soft, at least 3 minutes (again, the time will depend on the size and age of the peas).

The ideal thickness for soup is a matter of personal taste, so add water a little at a time.

While the peas are cooking, set up another bowl with ice and water. Transfer the pea mixture to a metal bowl or saucepan and **place the container in the ice water.** Stir the peas so they cool quickly.

Puree the soup in a blender for at least 3 minutes, **adding enough water to thin the soup,** about 1 cup. Press the puree through a fine sieve. Check the consistency and whisk in a little more water if you like. Season the soup with salt and pepper and serve hot or chilled.

parsnip soup

SERVES 6 TO 8

The recipe for this soup is so simple I am almost embarrassed to share it. It's a parsnip puree—that's it. No stock, just parsnips simmered in water, then pureed and seasoned. It's an opportunity for the ingredient to speak for itself and in doing so produce a remarkably complex and rich result. When you buy parsnips, choose firm unblemished ones. But for this recipe, don't worry too much if the cores are woody and fibrous because you boil the parsnips until they are soft and then pass them through a sieve. The stringy centers will not make it into the puree.

If you want to get fancy, you can steep complementary flavors with the parsnips. I've found that adding a vanilla bean or cardamom pods (tie them in cheesecloth to form a sachet) works well.

3 pounds parsnips, peeled and chopped

3½ quarts water

4 tablespoons (½ stick) unsalted butter, chilled and cut into small pieces

Kosher salt and freshly ground black pepper

Put the parsnips and water in a large pot. Season with salt and pepper and bring to a boil over high heat. Reduce the heat and simmer until the parsnips are very soft, about 1 hour.

Puree the soup in a blender or food processor in batches, adding cold unsalted butter to each batch. Strain the soup through a fine sieve. Adjust the consistency with water and the seasoning with salt and pepper; serve warm.

versatile vegetable purees

It's obvious once you think about it, but the only difference between a soup and a vegetable puree is the amount of liquid. Add only a little water when you're pureeing parsnips, peas, asparagus, peppers, or zucchini, and you have a light, delicious sauce. In professional kitchens, purees are used a lot to add color, flavor, and richness. Try stirring sweet pea or asparagus puree into a spring vegetable risotto. Purees are easy to make, freeze well, are full of vitamins, and offer an easy, healthy way to make simple meals more sophisticated.

Whether a puree is the starting place for a soup or a sauce, I like to strain it. You don't have to, but I do because I like the refined texture you get. If you are going to strain, I suggest you set two pots or containers next to the blender, one to use as you strain and the other to hold the finished soup or sauce.

yellow pepper soup

SERVES 6 TO 8

This is a soup I learned to make in Florence while I was working at Cibrèo. Made with vegetables and water, it is amazingly rich without the addition of meat or stock. Potatoes thicken the soup. Use a yellow variety like Yukon Gold. They have just the right amount of starch to make a velvety puree.

If you have Blond Soffritto Base (page 12), heat ½ cup in a large pot and then begin following the recipe when the peppers are added.

Peppers that are a very deep uniform yellow (no green streaks) are at the peak of ripeness and are sweeter.

½ cup extra virgin olive oil plus additional for finishing the soup

½ cup minced onion

¼ cup minced carrot

¼ cup minced celery

3½ pounds yellow peppers (about 7), cored, seeded, and chopped

2 pounds Yukon Gold potatoes (3 medium), peeled and chopped

2 fresh or dried bay leaves

About 9 cups water

Kosher salt and freshly ground black pepper

½ small bunch of thyme, tied in a bundle

Heat the oil over medium-high heat in a large pot. Add the onion, carrot, and celery and fry, stirring frequently, until the soffritto vegetables soften and color slightly, about 10 minutes.

Add the peppers to the pot and cook, stirring to coat them thoroughly with soffritto. Cook the peppers until they soften a little, 3 minutes or so, then add the potatoes and stir to mix all the vegetables together.

Add the bay leaves and enough water to come about an inch over the vegetables. Season with salt and pepper and bring the soup to a boil. Simmer until the peppers and potatoes are almost soft, about 30 minutes.

Bruise the thyme by crushing it with the flat side of a knife and then add it to the pot. Continue to simmer the soup until the peppers and potatoes are completely soft, about 15 minutes more.

Remove the thyme and bay leaves. Puree the soup in batches in a blender or food processor, incorporating ½ cup more oil for additional richness, if desired. Strain the soup through a fine sieve, adjust the seasoning with salt and pepper, thin with water if necessary, and serve warm with croutons and thyme leaves, if desired.

zucchini and basil soup

SERVES 6 TO 8

Look for small zucchini to make this, as they're a little sweeter. It's essential that once the zucchini goes into the pot that the temperature stays high to lock in the color and keep the taste sharp. Add the zucchini a little at a time to maintain the heat in the pot.

If you must use larger zucchini, remove the seeds.

If you have Blond Soffritto Base (page 12), heat ½ cup in a large saucepan, then follow the recipe where the zucchini is added.

To toast pine nuts, put them in a single layer in a dry skillet and cook over medium-low heat, stirring once or twice, until the pine nuts begin to color, about 3 minutes.

Cut the zucchini small to ensure it cooks quickly and make sure the water is boiling when you add it.

3 pounds small zucchini, trimmed, or 3½ pounds medium zucchini, trimmed and seeded

⅓ cup extra virgin olive oil plus additional for serving

½ cup minced red onion

¼ cup minced celery

¼ cup minced carrot

Kosher salt and freshly ground black pepper

About 5 cups boiling water

1 cup loosely packed basil leaves

¼ cup toasted pine nuts

½ cup toasted croutons

About 2 tablespoons freshly grated Parmigiano-Reggiano

Cut the zucchini into quarters lengthwise, then slice thinly. Reserve the chopped zucchini.

Heat the oil in a large pot over medium-high heat. Add the onion, celery, and carrot and fry, stirring frequently, until the soffritto vegetables begin to soften (you don't want them to color), about 5 minutes.

Raise the heat to high. Add the chopped zucchini, a little at a time, stirring to coat it with the soffritto. Season with salt and pepper and cook until the zucchini begins to soften, about 3 minutes.

Add enough boiling water to cover the vegetables by an inch. Allow the soup to boil gently until the zucchini is tender, about 8 minutes. Add the basil. Cook until the basil is wilted and bright green, less than 1 minute.

Puree the soup in batches, then pass it through a fine sieve. Adjust the seasoning with salt and pepper. Serve the soup warm garnished with pine nuts, croutons, and Parmigiano and drizzled with oil.

chilled asparagus soup with ramps

SERVES 4

This is the ultimate spring soup. To make it, you follow the same procedure as the Sweet Pea Soup (page 76), except you don't need to blanch the asparagus. You also need a little less water to thin the soup, as asparagus is much less starchy than peas. I use ramps (wild leeks) because they have a subtle garlicky bite I like. Ramps are available only a few weeks a year and are most often found at farmers' markets. If you can't get them, use leeks or shallots.

3 tablespoons unsalted butter
1 cup thinly sliced ramps (both whites and leaves sliced but kept separate)
Kosher salt and freshly ground black pepper
4 cups thinly sliced asparagus (about 2 pounds)
3 cups boiling water

Melt the butter in a large deep skillet over medium-low heat. Add the white parts of the ramps and season with salt and pepper. Cover and sweat them (cook in their own juices until they are soft but not yet beginning to color), about 7 minutes.

Add the asparagus. Stir to coat with the butter and cook until the asparagus turns a brighter green, about 3 minutes. Add salt, pepper, ramp leaves, and the boiling water. Cook over high heat until the asparagus is soft, about 3 minutes.

While the asparagus is cooking, set up an ice bath (for more on this, see the second note on page 76). Transfer the asparagus, ramps, and their cooking liquid to a metal bowl or pot and cool in the ice bath. Stir the mixture so it cools as quickly as possible.

Puree the soup in a blender for at least 3 minutes. Press the soup through a fine sieve. If it is too thick, whisk in a little more water. Season the soup with salt and pepper. Serve chilled. The soup may separate as it sits in the refrigerator. Just whisk it to bring it back together and always taste to make sure the seasoning is correct.

Ramps are good lots of different ways. The whites are a nice substitute for onions or leeks and are excellent roasted and pickled. The young leaves are great torn into salads or sautéed with greens.

Cut the asparagus as small as you can. If you are using pencil or regular size, thinly slice each spear, stopping short of the tough end. If you are using larger spears, cut the asparagus in half lengthwise first.

stracciatella

SERVES 6

My family always starts Easter dinner with this Italian egg drop soup. Start with good homemade broth, use a small deep saucepan (you don't want the egg to spread over too large a surface area), and use a good Parmigiano—aged 3 years—it makes a difference.

- **3 large eggs**
- **2 tablespoons freshly grated Parmigiano-Reggiano plus additional for serving**
- **1 tablespoon finely chopped fresh flat-leaf parsley**
- **Pinch of freshly grated nutmeg**
- **Kosher salt and freshly ground black pepper**
- **4 cups Easter Broth (page 8) or other rich homemade broth**

Beat the eggs and then mix in the Parmigiano and parsley. Season the egg mixture with nutmeg, ½ teaspoon salt, and ½ teaspoon pepper.

Bring the broth to a rolling boil in a small deep pot over high heat. Turn off the heat and add the eggs all at once. Immediately cover the pot and allow the steam to cook the eggs for 5 minutes. Do not stir.

Remove the lid and then, using a small whisk, gently break the egg into strands or "little rags" (the literal translation of stracciatella). Adjust the seasoning if necessary, then ladle the soup into bowls and serve immediately with Parmigiano.

This soup is completely dependent on the quality of the broth you use. If you don't have good homemade broth, wait to make it until you do.

My Zia Leda taught me to get the broth really boiling—let it go at least 3 minutes so you're really sure it's hot. Then turn off the heat, pour the egg into the broth, cover the pot, and walk away. Never stir the egg. After about 5 minutes, use a whisk to gently break the egg into strands.

chicken soup with escarole, farro, and dumplings

SERVES 6 TO 8

Odd as it may seem, the inspiration for this soup was not a cherished family recipe but canned Progresso Chickarina Soup. I loved it as a child, and when I opened Hearth, I wanted to make my own version. The dumplings, really tender chicken meatballs, are poached in broth, and I added escarole and farro to my notion of the original recipe. It's a very soothing soup and not hard to make, but be aware that the quality of the broth is key.

FOR THE DUMPLINGS:

- 1 pound ground chicken
- 1 egg
- 2 teaspoons very finely chopped fresh rosemary
- ⅓ cup freshly grated Parmigiano-Reggiano
- ¼ teaspoon freshly grated nutmeg
- Kosher salt and freshly ground black pepper
- ¼ cup heavy cream

FOR THE SOUP:

- 2 tablespoons extra virgin olive oil plus additional for serving
- 2 cups diced onions
- 1 cup diced carrots
- 1 cup diced celery
- Kosher salt and freshly ground black pepper
- 1 medium head of escarole, wilted leaves and core discarded, leaves chopped
- 12 cups Easter Broth (page 8) or other rich homemade broth
- 2 cups cooked farro (page 102)
- Freshly grated Parmigiano-Reggiano

Really clean the escarole. Chop it and then put it in a big container of water. Soak the escarole for several minutes and then gently lift it out of the water (leaving the grit behind). Rinse out the container and repeat at least twice.

(recipe continues)

I think piping the dumplings out is the way to go, but you could also drop teaspoonfuls of the chicken mixture into the broth.

TO MAKE THE DUMPLINGS: Place the chicken, egg, rosemary, Parmigiano, and nutmeg in a food processor. Season with salt and lots of pepper and pulse until mixed, adding the cream gradually. Spoon the mixture into a piping bag or a resealable plastic bag (if you snip a corner, this will work just as well). Chill the dumpling mixture.

TO MAKE THE SOUP: Heat the oil in a large pot over medium heat. Add the onions, carrots, and celery. Season with salt and pepper and mix well. Cover and sweat the vegetables (cook them until they are soft but have not yet begun to color), stirring occasionally, about 10 minutes.

Add the escarole, stir to coat with oil, reduce the heat to low, and cook, stirring occasionally, until the escarole starts to wilt, about 5 minutes.

Add the broth and farro. Bring the soup to a boil over high heat. Once again lower the heat. Simmer until the escarole is very soft, about 20 minutes. Season with salt and pepper.

Squeeze small dumplings (about the size of your thumb tip) from the bag into the simmering broth. Cover the pot and let the dumplings poach until they are firm, 10 minutes. Serve topped with Parmigiano, lots of black pepper, and oil.

The soup will keep in the refrigerator for days and freezes beautifully.

escarole soup

SERVES 4

All but the youngest escarole is too tough for salad, but the bitter leaves are perfect for soup—a fact not lost on the Italians, who use them in many classic preparations. This soup is the simplest and perhaps consequently the most elegant of them all. The escarole is just simmered in very good home-made broth. It couldn't be easier, but you do need to let the escarole cook for a good half hour, at which point the greens become soft and luscious while retaining their slightly sharp earthy flavor.

6 cups Easter Broth (page 8) or other rich homemade broth

1 medium head of escarole, wilted leaves and core discarded, leaves chopped

Kosher salt and freshly ground black pepper

About ½ cup freshly grated Parmigiano-Reggiano

About ¼ cup extra virgin olive oil

Bring the broth to a simmer in a large pot. Add the escarole. Season lightly with salt and pepper and simmer until the escarole is tender, about 30 minutes. Adjust the seasoning and serve topped with Parmigiano and oil.

Good broth is critical to the success of this soup.

Really clean the escarole. Chop it and then put it in a big container (or work in batches). Soak the escarole for several minutes, then lift it out of the water, leaving the grit behind. Rinse out the container and repeat at least twice.

ribollita

SERVES 8

When I opened Hearth, I made myself a couple of promises. First, from the beginning of fall to the end of winter, ribollita would always have a spot on the menu. And second, no matter what else goes on, I'd make sure to cook the first batch every year myself. It's a little nuts how much I love making that first huge pot each season. For me, this soup is perfection in a bowl. Healthy, tasty, deep, and complex without being fussy—it exemplifies what I find irresistible about Tuscan cooking.

Needless to say, I think you should try this recipe and make a big batch— ribollita only gets better when it's reheated. The only difficulty you may run into is finding black cabbage (also known as dinosaur kale or cavolo nero). It has a distinctive earthy flavor that makes a huge difference. Although you can substitute green kale, I think it's worth looking for black cabbage at farmers' markets or local Italian grocers (and it's been popping up more frequently at grocery stores).

About 2 tablespoons extra virgin olive oil
    plus additional for serving

3 cups diced onions

3 cups diced carrots

3 cups diced celery

Kosher salt and freshly ground black pepper

4 cups chopped savoy cabbage (about 1 small head)

⅓ cup plus 1 tablespoon tomato paste

8 cups finely chopped black cabbage (about 4 bunches)

10 cups Easter Broth (page 8) or water

5 cups cooked cannellini beans (page 117)

Thin toasted crostini (page 189)

Freshly grated Parmigiano-Reggiano

Fresh thyme leaves

You want the black cabbage to disperse throughout the soup, almost like an herb, so you have to chop it small. Here's Fabio Picchi's ingenious method: Cut out the tough spines, then freeze the leaves in plastic bags overnight. When you crush the frozen cabbage, it winds up in a million little pieces— just what you want.

Heat a skim of oil, about 2 tablespoons, in a large pot over medium heat. Add the onions, carrots, and celery. Season with salt and stir to coat the vegetables with oil. Cover and sweat the vegetables (cook without coloring), stirring occasionally, until they begin to soften, about 10 minutes.

Add the savoy cabbage. Mix well and cook, covered, until it begins to wilt, about 3 minutes.

Stir in the tomato paste, taking care to distribute it evenly. Turn the heat to low and add the black cabbage. Mix well, cover the pot, and **stew the vegetables until they are tender, about 20 minutes.** Add the broth or water, raise the heat, and bring the soup to a boil.

While the soup is cooking, **puree 3 cups of the beans in a blender or food processor, adding a little water if necessary.** Whisk the puree into the soup. Add the remaining 2 cups of beans and bring the soup back to a boil. Reduce the heat again and gently simmer, uncovered, until the flavors blend, about 30 minutes.

Season the soup with salt and lots of pepper. At this point, the soup can be cooled and refrigerated or frozen. To serve, ladle hot soup into bowls. Top each serving with crostini, Parmigiano, pepper, thyme leaves, and a drizzle of oil.

Notice that I don't add any liquid for quite a while; the vegetables stew in their own juices. This gives the finished soup very potent flavor.

How thick and full of beans you want your soup is a matter of personal taste. I like this heartier version in the winter. In the summer, I like a brothier soup and cut back on the beans and puree. I also vary the vegetables to suit the season, adding string beans, zucchini, and other squash when they are available locally.

salads

how to clean greens and herbs

Gritty, bruised, or damp lettuce can ruin a salad, and for me the whole meal. Washing greens is an unsung kitchen task that makes all the difference, but because it seems so simple, nobody ever tells you how to do it right. Here's my method.

- If the greens are ultimately going to be chopped, chop them before you wash them.

- Put the chopped, torn, or simply trimmed greens into a container large enough to hold them with at least 3 inches to spare. If you use the sink, make sure it is really clean. Or use a large pot or bowl. Work in batches if you need to.

- Fill the container with water. The greens will float. Mix them up gently, then let them sit for 2 minutes so the grit has time to settle.

- Gently lift the greens out of the water, leaving the grit behind. Place them in a colander. Drain the sink or container and wipe it out. Fill it once more with water and add the greens. Move the greens around in the water and again let them sit for a couple of minutes. Repeat until the greens are clean, at least two times (taste a leaf to be sure).

- Lift the greens out of the water a final time and dry them in small batches in a salad spinner. Spin them dry, then wrap them in a clean dish towel until you're ready to use them.

vinegar to taste

Making a well-dressed salad is a tricky balancing act. You want the acidic notes in the dressing to complement the richness and fruitiness of your oil. And you want well-chosen greens or vegetables to be coated just the right amount—not swimming in dressing and not naked.

The conventional wisdom is that vinaigrette should be made with one part vinegar for every three or four parts of oil. But I find that while sometimes that proportion hits the mark, other times it's just wrong. Rather than relying on a specific prescription, it's better to begin with the assumption that the proportions of oil and vinegar are a matter of taste and will vary depending upon the ingredients in your salad and the types of oil and vinegar you're using.

A dressing made with balsamic vinegar is best made with proportionately less oil. Balsamic is a little sweet as well as tart and rich in both taste and texture, so you need less oil to smooth the rough edges. I like my dressing a little acidic, so I often add a little kick with a squeeze of lemon juice just before serving.

insieme salad

A salad made with a single type of lettuce, freshly picked and simply dressed, can be delicious. But a salad made with a mixture of lettuces and vegetables, a combination of flavors and textures, can be amazing. At Insieme, we add very thinly sliced radishes and celery for bite and crunch to our mixed salad and top it with shaved Parmigiano-Reggiano.

We also garnish each plate with a seasonal selection of prepared vegetables. In the fall, we might use roasted beets, a little roasted cauliflower tossed with raisins and pine nuts, and maybe some roasted delicata squash. In the summer, it might be marinated eggplant, tomatoes, and baby zucchini. I've roughed out a recipe for the salad but urge you to let the market dictate what you choose and let the season and your mood determine the garnishes (if any).

Our dressing is made of aged balsamic and very good olive oil. As always, the exact ratio of oil to vinegar depends on personal taste.

1 head of radicchio

1 head of Belgian endive

½ head of Boston lettuce

½ head of red leaf lettuce

3 celery stalks, thinly sliced

3 medium radishes, thinly sliced

About 2 tablespoons balsamic vinegar (preferably aged)

About 3 tablespoons extra virgin olive oil (the best you have)

Kosher salt and freshly ground black pepper

About 12 shavings of Parmigiano-Reggiano

Aged balsamic is quite thick, so if you whisk the oil in gradually, it will emulsify and can be made ahead of time. Supermarket balsamic will not hold an emulsification, so if that is your choice, make your dressing just before you serve the salad.

Tear and then wash the greens. Dry them gently but thoroughly in a salad spinner and put them in a salad bowl. Add the celery and radishes.

In a separate small bowl, mix the vinegar and oil, adjusting as necessary to suit your taste. Season the dressing and the salad with salt and pepper. Dress the salad. Toss gently and serve topped with the Parmigiano.

romaine with butternut squash, smoked bacon, and gorgonzola cheese

SERVES 4 TO 6

If you see crispy white frisée lettuce, use it instead of the romaine. Both stand up nicely to the rich dressing, but frisée adds an interesting texture and bitter edge.

1 large butternut squash, peeled and cut into 1" dice

2 tablespoons extra virgin olive oil

2 tablespoons honey

Kosher salt and freshly ground black pepper

¼ pound thick-sliced bacon

4 hearts of romaine lettuce

4 tablespoons crumbled Gorgonzola cheese

About 2 tablespoons cider vinegar

Preheat the oven to 350°F. Put the squash in a bowl with the oil and honey. Season with salt and pepper. Mix to coat and then transfer the squash to a baking sheet. Bake until tender, about 20 minutes. Allow the squash to cool to room temperature.

While the squash cools, cut the bacon into short strips about as wide as the bacon slices are thick—lardons. Put them in a large skillet and cook over medium heat, stirring occasionally, until the fat is rendered and the bacon is crisp, about 7 minutes. Set aside in the pan.

Put the squash in a large mixing bowl. Tear the lettuce into manageable pieces. Add the lettuce to the bowl with the squash.

Tilt the salad bowl and, using a fork, smear the Gorgonzola onto the exposed side of the bowl (toward the bottom). Season the lettuce and squash with salt and pepper and sprinkle with vinegar. With the bowl tilted, pour the warm bacon fat with the lardons over the cheese. Let the salad sit for a minute or so.

Using your hands, toss the salad to mix the lettuce and squash with the melty cheese. Keep at it until all the cheese is incorporated. Adjust the seasoning if necessary with salt, pepper, and vinegar and serve.

green bean and potato salad

SERVES 6

When I make this, one of my favorite summer salads, I like to keep things simple. I start the potatoes; when they're almost done, I add the beans to the pot and finish cooking everything together. However, this does take a bit of finessing as the cooking times for the potatoes and the beans vary. Garden-fresh haricots verts, or baby string beans, are going to take much less time to cook than larger beans. And cooking times for potatoes can vary even more, depending on the type you're using, their age, and how you cut them. The recipe below was created using small young potatoes and very fresh young green beans. Adjust the times to fit the vegetables you're using or, if you prefer, simply cook the potatoes in one pot and the beans in another.

> 3 cups quartered small skin-on new potatoes
>
> Kosher salt and freshly ground black pepper
>
> 3 cups trimmed and halved small young green beans
>
> 1 small red onion, peeled, halved, and very thinly sliced
>
> ½ cup coarsely chopped fresh flat-leaf parsley
>
> ¼ cup extra virgin olive oil
>
> About 1½ tablespoons red wine vinegar

Put the potatoes in a medium to large pot. Add salt and water to cover by several inches and bring the water to a boil over medium-high heat. Boil the potatoes until they are almost tender, about 12 minutes.

Add the beans to the same pot and cook them until both the beans and potatoes are tender, about 5 minutes. Drain the potatoes and beans and put them in a large mixing bowl. Add the onion and parsley.

Dress the salad with the oil and vinegar to taste while everything is warm; this way, the flavor penetrates better. Season to taste with salt and pepper, then mix well. Serve warm or at room temperature.

arugula, fennel, and white anchovy salad

SERVES 4 TO 6

I love how sometimes a dish can be born from frantic necessity rather than thoughtful effort—this salad is a perfect example. During one of the early days at Hearth, I got a call from my fish guy at 4 p.m. saying that the snapper that was supposedly coming on a second run was in fact not coming at all. Two hours 'til dinner service and I needed an appetizer. I came up with this salad—it's turned out to be a real winner. People love it, and the toughest critic I've ever encountered, my mother, says it's her favorite salad of all time.

White anchovies are key. Sometimes sold as boquerones, they're lightly pickled, not salted like canned anchovies (which will not work as a substitute). They're much milder tasting, less salty, and pleasantly acidic. They're available at gourmet stores, some fish markets, and online.

FOR THE VINAIGRETTE:

  1 tablespoon finely diced shallot

  ½ small garlic clove, grated

  About 1½ tablespoons sherry vinegar, preferably aged

  ½ cup extra virgin olive oil

  Kosher salt and freshly ground black pepper

FOR THE SALAD:

  1 small fennel bulb

  ¼ pound arugula

  8–12 Pickled Cipollini Onions (page 258), depending on size
    (also see Note)

  8–12 thin crostini (page 189), broken into pieces

  Kosher salt and freshly ground black pepper

  16 white anchovy fillets

TO MAKE THE VINAIGRETTE: Combine the shallot, garlic, and vinegar in a bowl. Gradually whisk in the oil. Adjust the amount of vinegar if necessary, then season to taste with salt and pepper.

TO MAKE THE SALAD: Discard any discolored outer layers of the fennel. Quarter it, core each quarter, and then slice it as thinly as possible (a mandolin works well for this).

Put the fennel in a mixing bowl. Add the arugula. Cut the onions in half and then pull them apart, separating the layers; add them to the salad. Add half of the crostini, season with salt and pepper, and then dress the salad—you'll need 3 to 4 tablespoons of the dressing.

Arrange the salad on a serving platter. Garnish with the anchovy fillets (split whole fillets in half) and the remaining crostini, then serve.

When making the vinaigrette, start with 1½ tablespoons of vinegar and then add more if, like me, you like your vinaigrette acidic.

To make a quick pickle, halve and then slice a red onion. Put the slices in a mixing bowl. Season with salt and a little sugar, then cover with a mixture of 4 cups red wine vinegar and 1 cup water. Let the onion stand in the vinegar mixture for 1 hour, then drain it. The drained, pickled onion will keep in the refrigerator about a week.

This recipe makes a little more vinaigrette than you'll need. The extra will keep in the refrigerator for several weeks—you might even consider doubling the recipe. Keep vinaigrettes in small jars. That way, they are easy to shake and use when needed.

fava bean and pecorino salad

SERVES 4

Although there is no substitute for favas, blanched green beans (cut into ¼" lengths) are also good combined with young pecorino.

Spring onions have a brighter, sharper flavor than scallions, but scallions work as a substitute.

Don't be afraid of the oil in this recipe; you want to be generous. In fact, I suggest that you do what we do at the restaurant and marinate the diced cheese with the onion, oregano, peperoncini, and pepper in olive oil overnight (stored like this, the cheese will keep for weeks). Just before serving, add the marinade with the cheese to the favas, adjust the acidity with vinegar and wine, and then garnish with parsley.

Fresh favas can be hard to come by and are always incredibly labor intensive to clean, but this simple salad with a piece of great crunchy bread makes all the trouble worthwhile. I like to use Pecorino Toscano, a young, slightly soft and fairly mild pecorino. Aged pecorino, which is much easier to find, is stronger and overpowers the delicate sweetness of fresh favas. If it's all you can get, cut back a little on the amount.

Kosher salt

3 pounds fava pods (about 2 cups shelled)

6 ounces Pecorino Toscano or other young pecorino cheese

¼ cup very thinly sliced spring onions (halved if large)

1½ teaspoons dried oregano, preferably Sicilian

Pinch of minced peperoncini or red pepper flakes

¾ cup extra virgin olive oil

About ¾ teaspoon cracked black pepper

About 1 tablespoon white wine vinegar

1 tablespoon dry white wine

3 tablespoons finely chopped fresh flat-leaf parsley

Bring a large pot of salted water to a boil. Meanwhile, shell the favas. Drop the beans into the boiling water and blanch until their skins loosen, about 3 minutes. Cool the favas in ice water, then peel them and put them in a large bowl.

Cut the pecorino into ¼" dice and add it to the bowl. Add the onions, oregano, peperoncini, oil, pepper, vinegar, wine, and parsley. Mix well, season to taste with salt, and serve.

about farro

Farro is a somewhat obscure and definitely underused grain with a chewy texture and a great earthy, almost sweet, malty flavor that I love. High in B vitamins and full of protein, farro is low in gluten, so people with wheat issues can generally tolerate it. You can find it vacuum-packed at specialty stores or order it by mail.

You can use farro pretty much any way you would rice. Serve it plain as a sustaining side dish, treat it like Arborio rice to make risotto-like farrotto, or add it to soup. From a cook's standpoint, farro is great because it stops absorbing liquid when it's tender—this means it doesn't turn to mush in the pot.

farro

To make about 5 cups of cooked farro, heat 2 tablespoons of extra virgin olive oil in a large pot over medium-low heat. Chop, then add 1 small onion, 1 small carrot, and 1 small stalk of celery. Season with salt and pepper and stir the vegetables to coat them with the oil. Cover the pot and lower the heat. Cook the vegetables until they soften, about 10 minutes.

Add 2 cups of farro. Stir to coat it with the oil and vegetable juices. Add enough water to cover by about ½ inch. Raise the heat and bring the water to a boil, then adjust the heat so the farro simmers.

Cook the farro until it is tender, about 20 minutes, adding more water if the pot looks dry. Remove and discard the aromatic vegetables. Serve warm as you would rice or at room temperature (see recipes on pages 104 and 105).

In the fall and winter, I like a heartier flavor, so I render some chopped pancetta or prosciutto and use the fat to brown rather than sweat the aromatic vegetables. You can also cook the farro in stock rather than water for a richer taste.

winter farro salad

SERVES 4 TO 6

Seasonal cooking is about using ingredients when they're available, and it's also about reacting to the way you feel at different times during the year. Both this salad and the one that follows use ingredients that are available year-round. Yet I tend to make this salad in the winter and the other in the summer. Why? This winter salad is sweeter and more robust. It goes well with hearty, deeply flavored dishes—we serve it with Grilled Quail (page 192) during the cold weather. My summer farro salad is a brighter, somewhat more acidic dish, perfect for a light dinner on a hot summer night.

1 cup diced carrot

1 cup diced leek

Kosher salt and freshly ground black pepper

2 tablespoons finely chopped fresh thyme

4 cups cooked farro (see "About Farro," page 102)

6 tablespoons extra virgin olive oil

About ¼ cup balsamic vinegar

Blanch the carrot and leek in a large pot of heavily salted water, cooking just until tender, about 3 minutes. Drain and cool in ice water.

Combine the carrot, leek, thyme, and farro in a bowl. Dress with the oil and vinegar to taste. Mix well and season to taste with salt and pepper.

summer farro salad

SERVES 4 TO 6

How you cut the vegetables for this should be guided by how refined you want your salad to be. When I make this to go with a steak for the family, I don't peel or seed the tomatoes. I just cut them into pieces that are more or less the same size. I don't bother peeling or seeding the cucumber either; I use English cukes and cut them into pieces about the same size as the tomatoes. On the other hand, when I serve this at the restaurant, I'm picky. I get rid of all the peels and seeds and cut the vegetables into a small dice—about the same size as the grains of farro. Either way, the salad works well with a nice piece of roasted meat or fish.

> 4 cups cooked farro (see "About Farro," page 102)
>
> 1 cup diced tomato
>
> 1 cup diced cucumber
>
> ½ cup diced red onion
>
> ¼ cup loosely packed chopped fresh basil
>
> 6 tablespoons extra virgin olive oil
>
> About 3 tablespoons red wine vinegar
>
> Kosher salt and freshly ground black pepper

Combine the farro, tomato, cucumber, onion, and basil in a bowl. Mix well, then dress with the oil and vinegar to taste. Season with salt and pepper and serve.

tuna, cannellini bean, red onion, and tomato salad

SERVES 4 TO 6

I try to get my family to Tuscany every summer. My folks have a wonderful farmhouse there in a small town called Fauglia. When we arrive, the gardens are always in full swing, the tomatoes ripe, the onions ready to dig. And there are fresh cannellini beans—a real treat. The first thing I do when we arrive is make a big bowl of this salad. Frankly, I'd be very happy eating it every day. The beans don't have to be fresh; the tomatoes do, but not falling-off-the-vines ripe. They're better when they're a little tart and have some crunch. And this is the time to pull out your best olive oil.

I use canned Italian tuna even when I make this at home in New York. It's more expensive, but it tastes better. If I don't have any, I just leave the tuna out and have a salad of beans, tomatoes, onions, and basil.

1 (7-ounce) can imported Italian tuna

4 small tomatoes, cored and cut into wedges

1¼ cups cooked cannellini beans (page 117) or rinsed canned beans

1 small red onion, peeled, halved, and very thinly sliced

¼ cup fresh basil leaves, coarsely chopped

2 tablespoons red wine vinegar

3 tablespoons extra virgin olive oil

Kosher salt and freshly ground black pepper

Combine the tuna, tomatoes, beans, onion, and basil in a large bowl.

Dress the salad with the vinegar and oil. Season with salt and pepper, then mix gently and serve.

vegetables
and beans

because I grew up eating Tuscan food at home, I don't think I ever looked at meals as necessarily defined by the protein—the meat, chicken, or fish served. Sometimes a stew or a roast was the lead in my mother's meal, but often as not meats were given supporting roles, and not infrequently omitted entirely in favor of egg dishes, salads, pastas, and risottos. Today, although I love a good steak, there is an excitement I feel both as a cook and a diner when I think about vegetables.

Part of the allure of vegetables is that there are so many different kinds and what's good keeps changing. It's almost embarrassing how excited I get when the first shelling beans and fat Romano beans show up at the market each summer, and then they disappear long before I've grown tired of them. I love it that every time I visit the farmers' market it's a little different. What's ripe keeps shifting, and farmers are cultivating so many vegetable varieties that even after cooking all these years, I routinely come across greens I've never tasted or kinds of potatoes or eggplant I haven't had.

Because vegetables play such an important role in my cooking, vegetable recipes are scattered throughout the book, among the soups, pastas, risottos, and salads. But there were still many favorites I wanted to share, so here I've focused on recipes where particular vegetables get to star. Among them are a number of side dishes as well as a few dishes I would serve as a separate course, and a couple that would make a fine meal. What they have in common is a reliance on Italian cooking techniques and sensibilities to develop flavor and build savor.

cauliflower sformato

SERVES 4 TO 6

A sformato is a soufflé-like custard that is baked and then unmolded before serving (sformare means to unmold). You can flavor sformato with virtually any vegetable puree—spinach is really good. This cauliflower sformato makes a great side dish for Thanksgiving dinner.

> **About 2 tablespoons unsalted butter**
> **About ¼ cup bread crumbs**

FOR THE BÉCHAMEL:
> **3½ tablespoons unsalted butter**
> **2½ tablespoons all-purpose flour**
> **2 cups whole milk**
> **Kosher salt and freshly ground black pepper**
> **Pinch of freshly grated nutmeg**

FOR THE CAULIFLOWER:
> **1 medium head of cauliflower**

FOR THE CUSTARD:
> **2 eggs**
> **1 cup freshly grated Parmigiano-Reggiano**
> **Kosher salt and freshly ground black pepper**

Generously butter an 11" × 9" baking dish. Coat the dish with bread crumbs.

TO MAKE THE BÉCHAMEL: Melt the butter in a high-sided, heavy-bottomed saucepan. Whisk in the flour and then the milk. Bring to a boil, whisking constantly. (Watch the pan, because the milk has a tendency to boil over.) When the sauce reaches a boil, stir and adjust the heat so it is actively simmering. Cook, stirring frequently, first with a whisk and then with a wooden spoon, until the sauce thickens, about 15 minutes. Season with salt, pepper, and nutmeg and keep warm over very low heat.

TO MAKE THE CAULIFLOWER: While the béchamel cooks, put the whole cauliflower in a large pot. Add about 1" of water. Cover the pot and steam over high heat until the cauliflower is soft, about 20 minutes. Take the cauliflower out of the pot and allow it to cool; cut it into quarters.

Squeeze each quarter of the cauliflower in a clean dish towel to get rid of as much moisture as possible. Put the squeezed cauliflower in a food processor and pulse (make the puree as smooth or coarse as you like—I tend to prefer some texture, but it's a matter of personal taste).

TO MAKE THE CUSTARD: Beat the eggs in a large bowl. Stir in the cauliflower puree and Parmigiano. Strain the béchamel through a fine sieve and add it to the cauliflower; mix well. Season the mixture with salt and pepper.

Preheat the oven to 350°F.

Spoon the cauliflower mixture into the prepared dish. Lightly bang the dish on the counter to distribute the filling evenly. Bake the sformato until it sets and browns a little, about 40 minutes. Remove from the oven and allow to rest for 5 minutes. Unmold and serve.

Once you get the cauliflower custard into the baking dish, get it right into the preheated oven. If you let the sformato sit, the bread crumbs will start to absorb liquid from the filling, increasing the chances the sformato will stick.

roasted cauliflower

SERVES 4

You want the florets all about the same size, but it's okay if there is some variation—you'll wind up with some pieces a little more brown than others.

> 1 medium head of cauliflower, broken into florets
> 3 tablespoons extra virgin olive oil
> 2 fresh rosemary sprigs
> Kosher salt and freshly ground black pepper

Preheat the oven to 400°F. Put the cauliflower and oil in a bowl. Pull the leaves from the rosemary sprigs and add them to the cauliflower. Add salt and pepper and mix well.

Arrange the cauliflower on a baking sheet. Roast the cauliflower until it is tender and golden, about 15 minutes. Serve warm.

canned peas stewed in butter with onions

SERVES 4

It seems kind of strange now, but when I was a kid one of my favorite vegetables was canned peas. My mother would grab a silver can of Le Sueur baby peas from the cabinet. She'd chop an onion and cook it in butter until it was soft, then add the peas and some salt and a good amount of freshly ground pepper—that was it. I loved it and still do.

> 4 tablespoons (½ stick) unsalted butter
> 1 medium onion, peeled and chopped
> 2 (15-ounce) cans baby peas, drained
> Kosher salt and freshly ground black pepper

Melt the butter in a medium skillet over medium heat. Add the onion and cook, stirring occasionally, until soft and translucent, about 10 minutes. Add the peas, heat them through, season with salt and pepper, and serve.

broccoli rabe with chiles and garlic

SERVES 6

When you buy broccoli rabe, look for dark green leaves and stems and florets that have formed but not yet opened. When you get home, pull off the leaves and blanch them first, then add the bud-topped stalks. This way, no part of the rabe gets overcooked.

2 bunches broccoli rabe

Kosher salt and freshly ground black pepper

Pinch of minced peperoncini or red pepper flakes

1 large garlic clove, peeled and sliced

3 tablespoons extra virgin olive oil

Trim the broccoli rabe by cutting off the bottom of each bunch and then separating the leaves from the flower-topped stems. Snap off and discard the thin stems attached to the leaves.

Bring a large pot of salted water to a boil over high heat. Plunge the leaves into the boiling water. When the water returns to a boil, remove the leaves from the pot with a slotted spoon, cool them in ice water, then drain them well in a colander. Add the stems to the boiling water and cook until almost tender, about 2 minutes; then take them out of the pot, cool in ice water, and add them to the colander to drain.

Combine the peperoncini, garlic, and oil in a large skillet and warm over low heat. When the garlic begins to color, about 2 minutes, add both the broccoli rabe leaves and flower-topped stems to the oil. Gently warm the rabe in the garlic-infused oil just until the stems are tender, about 5 minutes. Adjust the seasoning with salt and pepper and serve.

verduri fritti: tuscan pastella batter

MAKES ABOUT 2 CUPS

It wouldn't be a holiday in my house if you couldn't find my aunt, mother, or most recently my wife holding court at the stove, presiding over two big sauté pans and frying batch after batch of verduri fritti. Some vegetables, the tender ones, we fry raw; others, like cauliflower, have to be precooked. When you are frying a relatively tough raw vegetable like an artichoke, the oil needs to be just hot enough to crisp the batter gently while allowing time for the vegetable within to cook. You want your oil temperature a little higher if you are frying a precooked vegetable like cauliflower or something tender like sage leaves. Never crowd the pan. Verduri fritti are great hot, but if you can resist, try waiting 5 minutes. At room temperature, the vegetables are soft-crisp, and you can eat them faster and appreciate the taste of each vegetable more.

1½ cups all-purpose flour

Pinch of salt

2 tablespoons finely chopped fresh sage

1½ cups ice water

Combine the flour, salt, and sage in a mixing bowl. Gradually whisk in the ice water, a little at a time, until the batter is the consistency of melted ice cream (you may not need to add it all). The batter can be made several hours in advance.

Vegetables That Can Be Fried Raw

Artichokes, spiky top cut off, outer leaves removed, and stem peeled; cut into thin wedges

Asparagus, trimmed

Eggplant, sliced; quarter or halve first if large

Fresh porcini mushrooms, quartered or thickly sliced

Green beans, trimmed

Onions, peeled and sliced into rings

Sage leaves, whole

Zucchini flowers, stamen removed

Zucchini, sliced or cut into batons

Vegetables That Must Be Precooked Before Frying

Cardoons, trimmed, peeled, and cut into 2" lengths; blanch in water combined with 2 tablespoons flour

Cauliflower (see recipe on page 113)

Winter squash, roasted or steamed; peel and cut into thick slices

Yams, peeled and steamed or roasted; cut into thick slices

cannellini beans stewed with sage

MAKES 6 CUPS

My goal when I cook beans is to get every one soft throughout but keep each whole. It is not so easy. Some people (like me) swear by soaking the dried beans, while others maintain it's unnecessary. Everyone agrees you have to cook beans slowly, but there's no consensus about when to add salt (I do it when the beans are almost cooked).

In the end, I believe the single most important thing is starting with the right beans. Even though they are dried, age matters—old beans just don't cook right. Consider ordering from Rancho Gordo; that's where I get mine. They grow their own beans and indicate when they were harvested on the label.

> *If you ever run across fresh shelling beans, buy them. Shucking takes time, but it's very much worth the effort.*

1 pound dried cannellini beans

1 head of garlic

1 bunch of fresh sage

Kosher salt

Toasted bread (optional)

Extra virgin olive oil (optional)

Cracked black pepper (optional)

Soak the beans overnight in water to cover by at least 3".

The next day, drain the beans and put them in a very large pot. Add enough water to cover the beans by about 2". Slice the stem end off the garlic to expose the cloves. Add the garlic to the pot along with the sage.

Cook the beans gently over moderate heat, adjusting the temperature so the water bubbles just occasionally. When the beans are soft but not quite tender, season them with salt and continue cooking until they are soft and creamy but still whole. The time will vary. I start checking after about 30 minutes and find that they are sometimes done in 45 minutes, but can take an hour and a half. Serve the beans warm, on toasted bread, dressed with oil and pepper. Or cool them and store them in the refrigerator in their cooking liquid.

> *Storing cooked beans submerged in their cooking liquid prevents the skins from drying and cracking.*

variation:

Substitute 1 pound of chickpeas for the cannellini beans. Simmer as directed above, but expect the peas to take at least 1 hour.

braised artichokes

SERVES 4 TO 6

You might be surprised to find how useful a pot of braised artichokes can be. You can of course serve them warm or at room temperature as an appetizer or part of a mixed antipasto spread, but they're also great sliced into salads. Or try adding black olives to the braise and using it as a sauce for pasta; finish with an aged pecorino and a ton of good extra virgin olive oil. If you skip the cheese, "the sauce" works beautifully with fish. Once made and covered with oil, the artichokes will keep for several weeks in the refrigerator.

2 lemons, halved

4 large artichokes

½ cup extra virgin olive oil plus additional for serving

2 large garlic cloves, peeled and crushed

1 small peperoncini, minced

1 tablespoon dried oregano, preferably Sicilian

1 large onion, peeled, halved, and thickly sliced

2 fresh rosemary sprigs

Kosher salt and freshly ground black pepper

¼ cup dry white wine

½ tablespoon white wine vinegar

¼ cup Easter Broth (page 8), chicken broth, or water

Sea salt and cracked black pepper

Rubbing the artichokes with lemon as you cut them prevents browning, as does holding them in lemon water. The artichokes can be prepared up to a day in advance.

Squeeze the lemons into a large bowl and add about 2 quarts of water. Trim each artichoke, removing the stem, leaves, and choke and leaving only the bottom. As you work, rub newly exposed bits of the artichokes with a lemon half to prevent browning. Keep the trimmed artichoke bottoms in the lemon water until you are ready to cook them.

Put the oil, garlic, peperoncini, and oregano in a high-sided skillet and turn the heat on low. Gently warm the oil, cooking until the garlic softens and becomes fragrant, 3 to 5 minutes.

(recipe continues)

*In the restaurant,
I cover the pan of
artichokes with a circle
of parchment paper—it
breathes just enough.
At home, I use a lid set
slightly askew to get the
same effect.*

Add the onion and rosemary and stir to coat with the flavored oil. Season with salt and pepper and cook over low heat, stirring occasionally, until the onion just begins to soften, about 3 minutes.

Drain the artichoke bottoms and add them to the pan. Stir and cook over medium heat until the artichokes start to look less raw, about 5 minutes. Add the wine, vinegar, and broth or water. Raise the heat and bring the liquid to a boil, then reduce the heat once more to low. Simmer, partially covered, until the artichokes are tender, about 30 minutes.

Remove the pan from the heat and allow the artichokes to cool in the braising liquid. Serve warm or at room temperature dressed with oil and plenty of sea salt and cracked pepper.

a useful technique

Many vegetables are delicious braised in the same aromatic broth I use for the artichokes. Cauliflower, fennel, cipollini onions, carrots, zucchini, peppers—the list goes on. Serve warm or, even better, store the braised vegetables in the refrigerator so you have an "ingredient" that allows you to change up salads, pastas, risottos, braises, and stews.

another useful technique

Stewing with soffritto is another of my favorite ways to cook many vegetables. I stew romano beans (opposite) and black cabbage (page 126) the same way. It works equally well with regular old string beans, Chinese yard-long beans, savoy cabbage, green kale, and Swiss chard. Or try cauliflower, zucchini, or bell peppers. Pretty much any but the most delicate vegetables can be handled this way—just vary the amount of water you add and the time to suit your ingredient.

stewed romano beans

SERVES 6

The first day I see these broad, dense beans arrive at the green market each year is a very happy one, and I know this dish will appear on my table every summer until the day I die. Forget about what you may have learned about blanching beans quickly so they retain some crunch. These babies are cooked for a long time, and they become soft, army green, and addictively delicious.

1 cup extra virgin olive oil

½ cup minced celery

½ cup minced carrot

1 cup minced red onion

1 garlic clove, peeled and crushed

2 fresh rosemary sprigs

1 teaspoon tomato paste

4 whole peeled plum tomatoes (canned or fresh)

Kosher salt and freshly ground black pepper

1½ pounds Romano beans, stem ends trimmed and halved crosswise

½ cup water

If you have Blond Soffritto Base (page 12), start with ⅓ cup. Add the garlic and rosemary and follow the recipe from there.

Heat the oil in a large high-sided skillet over medium-high heat. Add the celery, carrot, and onion; cook the soffritto, stirring occasionally, until the vegetables are golden, about 15 minutes.

Add the garlic and rosemary and cook until fragrant, about 5 minutes. Add the tomato paste, mix well, and cook until it darkens slightly, about 2 minutes more. Using your hands, crush the tomatoes into the pan, allowing the juices within to fall into the pan. Season the soffritto mixture with salt and pepper. Reduce the heat and simmer, stirring occasionally, until the tomatoes blend into the soffritto, about 10 minutes.

Add the beans. Stir to coat them with the soffritto and add the water. Bring the liquid to a simmer. Season with salt, cover the pan, and reduce the heat to low. Gently braise the beans, stirring occasionally, until they are fully tender, about 45 minutes. Adjust the seasoning with salt and pepper and serve.

Add a little more water if the pan gets dry while the beans are cooking. Serve the beans warm, but don't throw out the leftovers; they're good the next day at room temperature.

zucchini frittata

SERVES 4

For some reason, people just don't think of serving eggs for dinner. I don't get it. A good frittata, filled with zucchini and onions, flavored with cheese, herbs, and olive oil, is a really comforting meal, and it's easy. Start with the right pan. If you have a large nonstick skillet, use it; if not, make sure your pan is well seasoned—you want things to go smoothly when you flip the frittata.

FOR THE FILLING:

> About 3 tablespoons extra virgin olive oil
>
> 4 cups zucchini sliced into rounds about ⅛" thick
>
> Kosher salt and freshly ground black pepper
>
> 1 medium yellow onion, peeled and sliced
>
> ½ cup coarsely chopped fresh basil

FOR THE BASE:

> 8 eggs
>
> ¼ cup whole milk
>
> 3 tablespoons extra virgin olive oil
>
> ¼ cup freshly grated Parmigiano-Reggiano
>
> ½ cup coarsely chopped fresh basil
>
> Kosher salt and freshly ground black pepper

This is one of the few times where overcrowding the pan is not a bad thing—it's actually a necessity. You need to start with a heap of vegetables because you'll wind up losing half of your original volume, leaving just the right amount of room for the egg mixture.

Start the vegetables over high heat—you want the moisture they release to evaporate on contact with the hot pan. Then adjust the heat when the vegetables are soft and taking on color, before you add the egg.

TO MAKE THE FILLING: Heat enough oil to coat the bottom of a large skillet, about 3 tablespoons, over high heat until wisps of smoke come off the oil. Add all of the zucchini. Season with salt and pepper, then pile the onion on top and season again.

Cook the vegetables without stirring until you begin to see some color on the edges of the zucchini, about 2 minutes. Once they begin to color, stir the vegetables and continue cooking, stirring occasionally, until they all soften and are nicely browned, about 15 minutes.

When the vegetables are tender (their volume reduced by about half), add the basil. Cook, stirring in the basil, until it is wilted, about 2 minutes.

Distribute the vegetables so they fill the pan in an even layer.

(recipe continues)

TO MAKE THE BASE: While the filling is cooking, mix the eggs, milk, oil, Parmigiano, and basil in a bowl. Season with salt and pepper.

Pour over the vegetables. Reduce the heat to medium-low. As the egg begins to set, use a spatula or fork to pull the edges away from the rim and poke holes across the center, allowing raw egg to fill in around the cooked vegetables.

Adjust the heat so the eggs are bubbling a little, between medium-low and medium. Continue to gently lift the set egg toward the center, allowing raw egg to run to the edges. Cook the frittata until there is no more runny egg, about 5 minutes. Turn the heat to low and let the frittata set a little more for about 3 minutes.

To flip the frittata, run a spatula around the edges to loosen the egg from the pan. Give the pan a good shake; the frittata should move as a whole. This assures you that it is not sticking. (If it is still wet, cover it and let it stand for 5 minutes. If it is sticking, take it off the heat and let it set for 5 minutes longer and then gently loosen the frittata from the pan with a spatula.)

Place a dinner plate over the skillet and turn the frittata over onto the plate. Slide the frittata back into the skillet and cook the second side over medium heat just until lightly golden, about 4 minutes more. Again run a spatula under the frittata and flip it onto a serving plate.

Allow the frittata to rest for at least 5 minutes, then serve warm or at room temperature. (I always make extra so there will be leftovers to eat in a baguette for lunch the next day.)

asparagus frittata

Substitute 2 bunches of pencil asparagus for the zucchini. Cut the tips from the asparagus and retain them. Cut the stems into $1/2$" segments. Cook the asparagus tips and stems with the onion and proceed as above.

scallion (or spring onion) frittata

Substitute 6 cups of sliced scallions (about 8 medium bunches), using about $2/3$ of each scallion (or an equivalent quantity of spring onions), greens and whites thinly sliced, for the zucchini and onion and proceed as above.

zucchini with tomatoes and parmigiano

SERVES 4 TO 6

This is the thing to make at the height of summer, when young zucchini and vine-ripened tomatoes are available. It's a homey dish—no layering or elaborate presentation here, really just a glorious sauté, made start to finish in one pan.

About 4 tablespoons extra virgin olive oil

2 pounds small zucchini, thinly sliced into rounds

1 large red or yellow onion, peeled, halved lengthwise, and sliced

Kosher salt and freshly ground black pepper

4 plum tomatoes, chopped

¼ cup coarsely chopped fresh basil

6 tablespoons freshly grated Parmigiano-Reggiano

Coat the bottom of a large skillet with about 3 tablespoons oil and heat over high heat. Add the zucchini and then cover with the onion. Cook the vegetables without disturbing them until you begin to see color on the edges of the zucchini, about 3 minutes. Add salt and pepper and stir the vegetables. Continue cooking until the zucchini and onion begin to color, about 15 minutes. Stir them so they brown evenly and add more oil if the pan looks dry.

Add the tomatoes and a little more salt and pepper and reduce the heat to medium. Cook, stirring frequently, until the tomatoes release their liquid, soften, and begin to break apart, about 10 minutes.

Add the basil and 2 tablespoons Parmigiano. Adjust the seasoning and serve topped with additional cheese.

Choose a pan that will just barely contain the zucchini and onion. A tight fit will ensure that during the first few minutes of cooking the vegetables steam as well as fry. As they cook, they will shrink and caramelize more readily. By the time they are brown, the volume will have reduced by about a third, leaving plenty of room for the tomatoes.

stewed black cabbage

SERVES 4 TO 6

Black cabbage (also known as cavolo nero or dinosaur kale) has an intensely earthy flavor that I really like. It's delicious on its own braised with soffritto for a very typical Tuscan side dish that's perfect with roast meat and poultry. For a more substantial dish, I've added chickpeas to the cabbage and served over polenta.

If you have Blond Soffritto Base (page 12), start with ½ cup and then add the tomatoes and follow the recipe from there.

½ cup extra virgin olive oil

1 cup minced red onion

½ cup minced carrot

½ cup minced celery

Kosher salt and freshly ground black pepper

5 whole peeled canned tomatoes

3 pounds black cabbage, ribs and stems removed, leaves chopped (about 12 cups)

2½ cups chickpeas, canned or cooked dried (see recipe variation page 117)

6 cups soft polenta (see recipe page 254)

Heat the oil in a large high-sided skillet over medium heat. Add the onion, carrot, and celery and fry, stirring occasionally, until the vegetables soften and color, about 15 minutes. Season the soffritto with salt and pepper.

Using your hands, crush the tomatoes into the pan, allowing the juices within to fall into the pan. Cook, stirring frequently, until the tomato juices evaporate, about 5 minutes.

If you go slowly and check the pot from time to time, you don't even have to add water—the greens throw off enough liquid to keep the braise moist.

Add the cabbage a handful at a time, mixing and allowing it to wilt before adding more. Season with salt and pepper (add a little water if the pan looks dry). Cover the pan and cook, stirring every 5 minutes or so and adding a tablespoon or two of water if the cabbage begins to look dry. Cook over low heat until the greens are tender, about 30 minutes. Add the chickpeas and heat through, about 10 minutes. Serve warm over polenta.

marinated roasted peppers

MAKES ABOUT 1 QUART

The goal here is tender skinless peppers. You can get there by roasting the peppers in the oven, but I prefer to char them over a gas stove burner. It's fast and gives the peppers a slight smoky taste. Interestingly, it is not the few minutes over the flame that softens the peppers; it's the time they spend in a sealed bowl or bag. Steam builds up within the peppers as they are charred. Allowing them to cool in a sealed environment gives the peppers a chance to cook and soften from within. Once they are peeled and covered with seasoned oil, the peppers will keep in the refrigerator for a week or so.

6 red or yellow bell peppers

Kosher salt and freshly ground black pepper

6 garlic cloves, peeled and sliced

18 fresh basil leaves

About 2 cups extra virgin olive oil

If you don't have a gas stove, you can get a similar effect by charring the peppers under the broiler. Keep an eye on them, turning them when the skins start to wrinkle and brown.

Place 2 peppers directly on each gas burner over a high flame. As the pepper skins begin to char, turn them gently with tongs, coloring them evenly all over, about 10 minutes.

Transfer the peppers to a bowl and cover tightly with plastic wrap. Allow the peppers to steam until they are cool enough to handle, about 20 minutes.

Remove the charred skin (this is most easily done by wiping the peppers with a clean towel). Avoid rinsing the pepper, as this washes away flavor. Cut away the stem and discard the seeds. Cut the peppers in half lengthwise, then lay each piece out flat and carefully trim off the white "ribs" on the inside. Rather than slice them, I like to separate the peppers by following their natural structure. They typically divide into three or sometimes four good-sized pieces.

Put a layer of peppers in the bottom of a quart container with a tight lid. Season them with salt and pepper, then scatter garlic and basil leaves on top. Repeat layering the peppers, garlic, and basil, then cover with oil. Store in the refrigerator.

eggplant caponata

SERVES 6 AS A FIRST COURSE OR SIDE DISH

My caponata is a riff on a classic. Balsamic vinegar's mellow, rich, sweet-and-sour flavor works with eggplant, which can be a little bitter, so I use it instead of the traditional wine vinegar, and I add thyme. Basil, mint, and rosemary also work, but I prefer thyme.

8 cups diced (about ¾" square) unpeeled eggplant
(about 2 medium)

Kosher salt and freshly ground black pepper

About 7 tablespoons extra virgin olive oil

1 large onion, peeled and diced

1 garlic clove, peeled and minced

¼ teaspoon ground cinnamon

2 tablespoons pine nuts

2 tablespoons golden raisins

1½ tablespoons chopped fresh thyme

1½ teaspoons sugar

2 tablespoons balsamic vinegar

¼ cup strained tomato puree (canned or Pomarola, page 18)

I salt the eggplant in this recipe because eliminating the moisture before frying allows the eggplant to brown and soften nicely during cooking.

Toss the eggplant with 2 tablespoons salt and set aside in a strainer for 20 minutes to drain. Pat the eggplant dry with paper towels or clean dish towels.

Heat about ¼" oil in a large skillet over high heat. When the oil starts to smoke, gradually start adding eggplant to the pan, adding only enough to almost fill the pan in a single layer. Cook the eggplant, turning it occasionally, until it begins to brown, about 5 minutes. Using a slotted spoon, transfer the browned eggplant to a plate lined with paper towels to drain. Add a little more oil and repeat, cooking the remaining eggplant; drain on paper towels.

Adjust the heat to medium-high, add more oil if the pan is dry (you want a good skim when you add the onion). Add the onion, season with salt and pepper, and cook until it softens slightly, about 1 minute. Add the garlic and cinnamon. Cook, stirring to prevent burning, for another minute. Add the pine nuts, raisins, and thyme. Continue cooking, stirring as you go, until the onion is soft and golden, about 5 minutes more.

Return the eggplant to the pan and add the sugar, vinegar, and tomato puree. Reduce the heat to medium, season again with salt and pepper, mix well, and simmer until the mixture reduces slightly and the flavors blend, about 15 minutes. Turn off the heat and allow the caponata to settle for at least 5 minutes. Serve warm, at room temperature, or chilled.

buying and cooking eggplant

Shape and size play a big role when I choose eggplant. I think about what I'm making and pick accordingly. If I want small rounds, I go for a long narrow variety; if I'm roasting and pureeing, I pick a larger type. No matter what, I look for a glossy, tight-skinned, heavy fruit—by "heavy," I mean for its size. If it's heavy in the hand, it's neither old nor full of seeds and it's not dried out. (This is a pretty good rule to follow with most fruits and vegetables.)

I salt eggplant—sometimes. I don't salt to change flavor or remove bitterness. I salt when I want to get rid of excess water. When I make an old-school, Eggplant Parmigiana, American Style (page 134), I salt because I don't want the parmigiana to be too wet. And because the skin helps eggplant slices to hold their shape (and also provides a nice color contrast), I leave it on mostly—whenever I want intact pieces for the grill or frying. I remove the skin when I want the eggplant to blend with other ingredients. For example, I peel it to steam lemon with herbs (see Eggplant in a Bag, page 138).

Eggplant is very absorbent, and frying it can be a particular challenge. Fry eggplant quickly in hot oil; adjust the heat if necessary and don't add the eggplant all at once. I like to put a piece or two in, get them going, and then add a few more, creating a rotation. When the first slices are fried, I replace them. This way, I wind up with slices of eggplant at various stages of doneness in the pan up until the end. I maintain as even a temperature as possible and can be more relaxed than if all my eggplant were ready at the same time.

summer eggplant parmigiana

SERVES 6

I first saw this dish prepared when I was working at Cibrèo in Florence. There young eggplant is fried but not breaded. It's layered with a little tomato and mozzarella, seasoned, and baked. The finished dish has a fresh character that makes it work at the height of eggplant and tomato season—when the weather is hot. One thing I should mention: Expect to find a good amount of liquid in the bottom of the pan when you spoon out the first serving of eggplant. The eggplant releases the olive oil it accumulates during frying. The oil mixes with the vegetable juices and creates a "jus" that I spoon over each plate (and sop up with bread).

Summer Parmigiana showcases young egg-plant, so pick carefully. Also buy the freshest mozzarella you can find.

4 small or 2 medium eggplant (about 1½ pounds)

Extra virgin olive oil for frying

Kosher salt and freshly ground black pepper

1 (28-ounce) can whole peeled tomatoes

1 tablespoon thinly sliced garlic

1 tablespoon dried oregano, preferably Sicilian

1½ cups freshly grated Parmigiano-Reggiano

¾ cup loosely packed fresh basil leaves

8 ounces fresh mozzarella, buffalo if available, diced

Preheat the oven to 350°F. Slice the eggplant into disks about ½" thick.

Heat about ½" oil in a large skillet over medium-high heat. When the oil is hot and just about to start smoking, begin to cook the eggplant in batches, adding oil as necessary. Cook until each piece is crisp and golden, 2 to 3 minutes per side. Drain the cooked eggplant on a plate lined with paper towels. Salt each batch while it is still hot.

Assemble the parmigiana in a medium baking dish (11" × 8"). Begin by crushing 3 tomatoes with your hands; let the juices fall into the pan and scatter the pieces evenly over the bottom. Season the tomatoes with a little garlic (about 7 small slices), a pinch of oregano, a little Parmigiano, salt, and pepper. Tear and scatter 4 basil leaves over the tomatoes, then cover with a layer of eggplant, fitting the rounds in snugly.

Top the eggplant with 2 more crushed tomatoes and a little less than one-third of the mozzarella. Season this layer like the last, with garlic, oregano, Parmigiano, salt, pepper, and basil. Cover with another layer of eggplant, then 2 tomatoes and another third of the mozzarella; season as before. Finish the parmigiana with a final layer of eggplant.

If you are using larger eggplant or have sliced yours more thinly, go ahead and make an extra layer—finishing the last most generously as described.

The last layer of tomato and cheese is the most generous. Crush the remaining tomatoes over the eggplant, cover with the remaining mozzarella, and season with the remaining garlic, oregano, Parmigiano, and basil; season with salt and pepper.

Bake uncovered until the cheese and "sauce" are bubbly, about 40 minutes. Remove the pan from the oven and let rest in a warm place for 15 minutes. Serve, spooning pan juices over each serving.

eggplant parmigiana, american style

SERVES 6

The eggplant parmigiana you find in most Italian restaurants in this country is probably more American than it is Italian, but who cares? When it's made right, it's delicious. The trick is getting the breaded eggplant crisp enough that it can hold its own after baking with sauce and cheese. A good Italian-American eggplant parmigiana is never watery, so you want to extract what liquid you can before you fry. I start by salting the sliced eggplant. I bread the slices simply by dipping them in egg and then bread crumbs mixed with a little cheese. This gives a soft crunch and a nice robust flavor.

4 small or 2 medium eggplant (about 1½ pounds)

Kosher salt and freshly ground black pepper

4 eggs

¾ cup freshly grated Parmigiano-Reggiano plus additional for serving

2 tablespoons water

About ¾ cup unseasoned bread crumbs

Olive oil for frying

2 cups Tuscan Tomato Sauce (page 19)

2½ cups coarsely shredded mozzarella

Slice the eggplant into disks about ½" thick. Arrange a layer of eggplant in a large colander. Sprinkle with a generous amount of salt and then top with another layer of eggplant. Continue salting the eggplant until it is all in the colander. Set the colander over a bowl or in the sink and allow the eggplant to "sweat" for at least 30 minutes.

Preheat the oven to 350°F.

Mix the eggs, 2 tablespoons Parmigiano, water, and a pinch of salt and pepper in a medium bowl. Mix the bread crumbs and 2 tablespoons Parmigiano in another medium bowl.

Wipe the eggplant slices dry. Using a fork, dip each slice into the eggs and then into the bread crumbs. Press the bread crumbs into place with your hands.

Heat about ½" oil in a large skillet over medium-high heat. When the oil is almost smoking, begin to fry the eggplant in batches, never crowding the pan. Cook the slices until they are golden and then flip them and brown the second side, about 3 minutes per side. Drain the fried eggplant on paper towels, seasoning each batch with salt and pepper while hot.

Assemble the parmigiana in a medium baking dish (11" × 8"). Spoon about ½ cup tomato sauce into the dish to moisten the bottom. Add a layer of eggplant. Trim the last few pieces so they fit into the pan. Sprinkle the eggplant with about 2 tablespoons Parmigiano and top with a little less than one-third of the mozzarella. Spoon a little more sauce on top and continue layering until you have used all the eggplant. The final layer of sauce and cheese should be the most generous.

Bake the parmigiana until the cheese is melted and the sauce bubbly, about 40 minutes. Remove the pan from the oven and let the parmigiana rest in a warm place for at least 10 minutes. Serve warm or at room temperature with additional Parmigiano.

It is important to press the bread crumbs into the eggplant with your hands so the crust adheres.

Cut the last few pieces of eggplant to fit the pan. Odd shapes are okay. Squeeze them into the corners so the parmigiana fits as snugly as possible.

grilled marinated eggplant

SERVES 4 AS A FIRST COURSE OR SIDE DISH

Marinated eggplant makes a great antipasto, alone or as part of a larger spread. It also works as an accompaniment to grilled meat and fish. However you serve it, I strongly suggest you make sure to save enough for a sandwich. Country bread with grilled marinated eggplant, prosciutto, and mozzarella—really, really good.

½ cup loosely packed fresh flat-leaf parsley leaves

2 tablespoons drained capers

1 medium garlic clove, peeled and sliced

½ teaspoon dried oregano, preferably Sicilian

¼ teaspoon minced peperoncini or red pepper flakes

¼ cup extra virgin olive oil

Kosher salt and freshly ground black pepper

1 medium eggplant (¾ pound), peeled and sliced about ⅓" thick

3 tablespoons balsamic vinegar

You could make the parsley mixture in a food processor, but I don't. I find hand chopping gives me the somewhat drier texture I prefer.

For this recipe, I don't salt or oil the eggplant; I grill it dry. This way, it has a nice chewy texture. I marinate the eggplant as soon as it comes off the grill so the flavor of the marinade penetrates.

Finely chop the parsley with the capers and garlic. Add the oregano and peperoncini and chop everything together. Put the mixture in a bowl, stir in the oil, season with salt and pepper, and reserve.

Preheat an outdoor charcoal or gas grill or a grill pan until smoking hot.

Put enough eggplant slices on the grill to cover it without crowding. Cook the eggplant until well marked, 3 to 6 minutes, then turn the slices over. Cook until tender, about 3 minutes more. Remove the eggplant from the grill.

Pour the vinegar into a shallow bowl. While still hot, dip each eggplant slice into the vinegar and set it aside on a plate. Continue grilling and dipping the eggplant until all the slices are cooked and seasoned.

Spoon 2 tablespoons of the parsley mixture onto a platter and spread it evenly with the back of a spoon. Arrange half of the grilled eggplant on the parsley in a single layer. Smear each slice of eggplant with more parsley. Place a second layer of eggplant on top and spread the remaining parsley on it. Cover the dish with plastic wrap and set aside to marinate at room temperature for about 2 hours (or refrigerate for longer). Serve at room temperature.

eggplant in a bag

SERVES 6

Some people get turned off by the idea of cooking eggplant in a plastic bag. I admit it's a long way from rustic farmhouse cooking, but the result is eggplant with a texture like silky custard. Cooking vegetables in a sealed environment with aromatic vapor is a technique well worth playing around with. It works with virtually any vegetable; see the recipe for Mushrooms in Parchment (page 147).

Use firm, young eggplant for this recipe, and be sure to peel it so the flavors penetrate and blend.

1½ pounds baby eggplant

Strips of peel from 2 lemons, white pith removed, very thinly slivered

¼ cup extra virgin olive oil plus additional for serving

¾ cup loosely packed fresh basil leaves plus additional for serving

1 garlic clove, peeled and crushed

Kosher salt and freshly ground black pepper

Salsa Verde (page 255) (optional)

Peel the eggplant and cut it into disks about 2" thick. Place the eggplant, lemon peel, and oil in a bowl. Bruise the basil leaves with the side of a knife blade (this releases the oils) and add them to the bowl. Add the garlic, season with salt and pepper, and mix well. Spoon the mixture into resealable plastic bags (the number will depend on the size of the bags). Seal the bags, pressing out as much air as possible.

Bring a pot of water to a gentle simmer. Turn the heat to low, add the bags, and cover the pot. Cook at a low simmer until the eggplant is soft but still holds its shape, about 30 minutes. Serve the eggplant warm or at room temperature, dressed with additional oil and chopped basil or Salsa Verde.

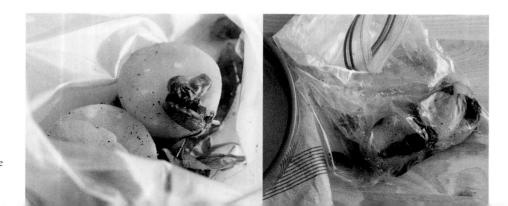

patate alla contadina

SERVES 4

This is Italian farmhouse cooking at its best. Your whole house smells good when you stew potatoes with tomatoes, garlic, herbs, and olive oil, and you wind up with a yummy mess of potatoes just beginning to fall apart. Use yellow potatoes like Yukon Gold, and feel free to play around. Olives, anchovies, and capers are all great additions. At Hearth, we add cauliflower, cabbage, or broccoli, a nice texture and flavor complement.

4 large Yukon Gold potatoes (about 2¼ pounds)

1 large garlic clove, peeled

5 whole peeled canned tomatoes

1 heaping tablespoon finely chopped fresh rosemary

⅓ cup fragrant extra virgin olive oil

Kosher salt and freshly ground black pepper

¼ cup water

4 tablespoons (½ stick) unsalted butter

Use good olive oil here because it is going to affect the flavor of the dish.

Cut the potatoes in half lengthwise, then lay each half flat side down and cut it into thirds crosswise (you'll wind up with thick half-moon slices). Put the potatoes in a bowl. Grate the garlic into the bowl. Crush the tomatoes with your hands and add them and their juice to the mixture. Then add the rosemary, oil, and generous amounts of salt and pepper. Mix well.

Grate the garlic so you don't wind up with chunks. I use a rasp.

Transfer the mixture to a medium saucepan and add the water. Cover and heat over medium-low.

You want the potatoes to steam, not fry or boil, so it is important that they are piled high and snug in a saucepan. Choose a smallish pot that is higher than it is wide and make sure it has a tight lid. And don't worry if the potatoes break a bit—this is a homey dish.

Bring the potatoes to a gentle simmer and cook for about 20 minutes. Give them a stir and continue cooking. Lower the heat if necessary (a gentle simmer is what you want) and stir every 10 minutes until the potatoes are soft, about 30 minutes more.

Mix in the butter. Adjust the seasoning if necessary with salt and pepper and serve.

tuscan fries

SERVES 4 TO 6

Cooking french fries is usually a two-step process: First you blanch the pota-toes in oil that is not too hot to get them cooked through, then you crank up the heat and refry them to get them crisp. The beauty of this Italian version is that by allowing the oil temperature to rise gradually, it all happens in one uninterrupted process. The other thing that distinguishes these fries is their unique shape. You want to pare quarter-size pieces from the potato. But you want angles. Use a paring knife to work your way around the potato, cutting off irregularly shaped but more or less uniformly sized bits. The fries have a great rustic look, and all the peaks and angles get extra-crispy.

3 russet potatoes, peeled
Olive or neutral-flavored vegetable oil for frying
1 large fresh rosemary sprig
Kosher salt and freshly ground black pepper

Peel and cut the pota-toes right before you cook them and don't hold them in water, which will rinse off that outer layer of starch that makes them crispy.

Begin to cut the potatoes with a paring knife into irregularly shaped, quarter-size pieces.

Meanwhile, heat about ½" oil in a large deep skillet over medium-high heat. When the oil is loose and shimmering, add the potatoes in a crowded layer. The potatoes will cool the oil, but the temperature will slowly come back up. Cook the potatoes without disturbing them until they are tender, about 20 minutes (you are cooking the inside of the potato at this point).

The potatoes get quite soft before they crisp and brown, so they break easily. Be patient and wait until you see a golden "skin" form before you move the po-tatoes, then turn them gently with a slotted spoon.

Once the oil temperature heats up again, you will see the potatoes begin to color. At this point, you want the oil hot but not smoking; adjust the tempera-ture if you need to. Then use a slotted spoon or spatula to move the potatoes around some—they have a tendency to stick to the pan and to one another. When they are pale gold, not quite done but getting near (about 10 minutes after they start to color), add the rosemary. Continue cooking until the potatoes are nicely browned, 5 to 10 minutes more. Transfer them to a plate lined with paper towels to drain. Salt and pepper the potatoes while they are hot and serve immediately.

marinated mushrooms

SERVES 4

This recipe is a perfect example of the kind of cooking that helps you to build a pantry—to create a versatile "ingredient" you can use to elevate simple meals. The marinated mushrooms are easy to make, and they keep in the refrigerator for weeks. Add them to salads, serve them over pasta, put them in sandwiches, or simply serve them warmed or at room temperature as a side dish with steak, chicken, or salmon.

When they are available, substitute wild mushrooms for the button mushrooms I use here or try using other cultivated varieties. You can mix different kinds as long as you pan-roast each variety separately.

1 pound button mushrooms, cleaned and stems trimmed

1½ teaspoons coriander seeds

About 6 tablespoons extra virgin olive oil

Kosher salt and freshly ground black pepper

4 tablespoons balsamic vinegar

1 heaping teaspoon finely chopped fresh thyme

½ teaspoon dried oregano, preferably Sicilian

Strips of peel from 1 lemon, white pith removed

Remember that the seasoning will become more concentrated as the mushrooms cook down (see "About Mushrooms").

Cut large mushrooms into quarters and medium mushrooms in half; leave any small mushrooms whole.

Toast the coriander seeds in a dry medium skillet over medium heat until fragrant, about 3 minutes. Transfer them to a cutting board and crush with the flat of a knife blade or pulse a few times in a spice grinder; set aside.

Heat a skim of oil, about 2 tablespoons, in a large skillet over high heat. When the oil slides easily across the pan, add about half of the mushrooms. Sprinkle with a little salt. Cook the mushrooms, turning them every so often. Initially they will release a lot of liquid. This will evaporate quickly in the hot pan, and the mushrooms will begin to brown. Add a little oil if the pan looks dry. Cook the mushrooms until they are golden, about 10 minutes. Add 2 tablespoons vinegar to the skillet. Turn the mushrooms in the vinegar, then transfer them to a bowl. Wipe out the skillet and repeat, cooking the remaining mushrooms in the same fashion. Add the second batch of mushrooms to the first.

Add the coriander, thyme, oregano, and lemon peel to the mushrooms. Add 2 tablespoons oil and season with salt and pepper. Mix well and set aside at room temperature for at least 30 minutes to marinate. The mushrooms will keep in a covered container in the refrigerator for weeks.

about mushrooms

Cooking mushrooms is, to a large extent, a matter of managing the release of moisture. While all mushrooms contain a significant amount, some varieties are wetter than others. Wild mushrooms tend to contain more moisture than cultivated, but can vary greatly based on the weather at the time they were picked. Of the cultivated varieties, shiitakes, portobellos, and oyster mushrooms are all relatively dry, while button and cremini are very moist. This doesn't mean you *can't* brown button and cremini varieties; it just means you'll need a really hot pan, space between the mushrooms, and more time. When moisture is released, it will hit the hot skillet surface and more or less immediately evaporate, never pooling around the mushrooms and causing them to stew in their own liquid.

Adding salt helps draw moisture from the mushrooms, but don't overseason. Remember that the mushrooms are going to shrink a great deal during cooking—60 percent or more. What seems like the right amount of seasoning at the beginning of cooking (when the mushrooms are still full of water) can wind up being too much. My best advice is to start out pan-roasting mushrooms in small batches over medium to high heat, leaving lots of room in the pan and seasoning lightly. If, as you cook the mushrooms, you find that they brown easily without releasing much liquid, you can take more liberties with batch size.

I should say that although mushrooms can be wet and you don't want to add to the problem, they also need to be clean. Gritty mushrooms are up there with gritty lettuce among the things that can most quickly ruin a meal for me. So my rule is: *If* you can eliminate *all* the grit by wiping the mushrooms with a dry cloth, do so. But I find that this is not usually enough. When it's not, don't hesitate to put them in a tub of water for a minute. But don't let them soak, and do dry them before they go into the pan.

mushrooms trifolati

SERVES 4

I pan-roast mushrooms in the same way for Marinated Mushrooms (page 144).

This is an easy classic. Pan-roasted mushrooms are flavored with garlic, peperoncini, and parsley. Serve this as a side dish for roasted meats or over warm polenta. Don't limit yourself to the button mushrooms used here; porcinis or a mixture of wild and cultivated mushrooms cooked this way are really good. Pan-roast the mushrooms up to a couple of hours ahead, cooking different varieties separately, then finish them together right before serving.

2 tablespoons chopped fresh flat-leaf parsley

1 large garlic clove, peeled

Pinch of minced peperoncini or red pepper flakes

1 pound button mushrooms

About 7 tablespoons extra virgin olive oil

Kosher salt and freshly ground black pepper

Finely chop the parsley with the garlic and peperoncini. Set aside.

Rinse and dry the mushrooms. Trim off the tough stem bottoms. Cut large mushrooms into quarters and medium mushrooms in half; leave any small mushrooms whole.

Initially the mushrooms will release a lot of liquid. This will evaporate quickly in the hot pan, and the mushrooms will begin to brown. Add a little oil if the pan looks dry.

Heat a skim of oil, about 2 tablespoons, in a large skillet over high heat. When the oil slides easily across the pan, add about half of the mushrooms and a little salt and pepper. Cook the mushrooms, turning them every so often, until they are golden, about 10 minutes in all.

Wipe out the skillet and repeat with the remaining mushrooms, adding another tablespoon or so of oil.

The mushrooms can be pan-roasted up to 2 hours ahead, then reheated with the parsley mixture just before serving.

Combine the parsley mixture with 3 tablespoons oil in a large skillet. Turn the heat to medium-high and allow the flavor of the parsley mixture to infuse into the oil. When the garlic is fragrant, about 2 minutes, add the pan-roasted mushrooms. Toss the mushrooms, mixing them with the parsley mixture. Cook the mushrooms until they are heated through, tossing or stirring frequently, about 3 minutes. Serve the mushrooms warm or at room temperature.

mushrooms in parchment

SERVES 4

I like the results you get from steaming in sealed parchment, relying on natural juices for flavored vapor. The flavors mingle as everything heats together in the parchment. I like to bring the sealed packets to the table and open them there—the smell is pretty intoxicating.

About 5 tablespoons extra virgin olive oil

2 pounds mixed wild and cultivated mushrooms, cleaned and stems trimmed, thickly sliced if large

2 fresh rosemary sprigs plus 1 teaspoon picked leaves

2 fresh thyme sprigs plus 1 teaspoon picked leaves

Kosher salt and freshly ground black pepper

1 garlic clove, peeled and thinly sliced

About 1 tablespoon aged balsamic vinegar

You can substitute 8 large porcini mushrooms for the wild and cultivated mushrooms. Thickly slice or quarter the mushrooms and then proceed as directed.

Preheat the oven to 400°F.

Place a baking sheet in the oven to get hot. Heat a skim of oil, about 2 tablespoons, in a large skillet over high heat. Add about half of the mushrooms, 1 rosemary sprig, and 1 thyme sprig; season with salt and pepper. Cook, stirring occasionally, until the mushrooms color, about 3 minutes. Transfer the mushrooms to a plate. Wipe out the skillet and repeat, cooking the remaining mushrooms in the same fashion. Discard the rosemary and thyme sprigs after pan-roasting the mushrooms.

Cut four large (16" × 12½") pieces of parchment and fold each in half. Cut each piece into a large half-oval. Unfold the parchment and mound mushrooms in the center of half of each piece. Season with garlic, olive oil, vinegar, salt, and pepper. Sprinkle with rosemary and thyme leaves and fold the paper to form packets.

If you don't have parchment, you can form packages out of foil. Just crimp the edges to seal.

To seal the packets, crimp and tightly pleat the edges, starting at one end of the fold. Seal the corner by folding it several times. Place the packages on the heated baking sheet and bake until the mushrooms are fragrant, about 5 minutes. Serve in the parchment directly from the oven.

If you can't get it sealed, staple the final corner shut.

braised morels

SERVES 6

This interesting technique is more French than Italian, but it's worth knowing about. The morels are braised in beurre fondue: an emulsified butter sauce. As the mushrooms cook, they slowly flavor the braising liquid, which then becomes a wonderful sauce. Serve the morels and sauce with roasted or poached chicken or fish (or even a steak) and you instantly have an elegant meal. Or toss fresh pasta with the mushrooms and sauce; add some Parmigiano and a grind of black pepper—life doesn't get much better. Just remember to start off with enough liquid in the pan and add the butter gradually. You're making an emulsion, and you need the right proportion of liquid to fat.

Butter-poaching is a delicious way to cook many different vegetables; try peas, asparagus, or sugar snaps. Parboiled lobster is also wonderful finished in beurre fondue.

1 pound fresh morel mushrooms, stems trimmed

2–3 tablespoons water

12 ounces (3 sticks) cold unsalted butter, diced

Kosher salt and freshly ground black pepper

1 fresh thyme sprig

Clean the morels by soaking them in a large pot of cold water; agitate and then let sit for 5 minutes. Gently lift the mushrooms out of the water and spread them in a single layer on paper towels to dry. Don't worry if they're a little damp—it's okay when you're cooking them this way. Cut any particularly large mushrooms in half.

Bring the water to a simmer in a medium saucepan over medium heat. Reduce the heat to medium-low. Whisk the butter into the simmering water one piece at a time. Season with salt and pepper and then add the mushrooms, stirring to coat them with the sauce. Don't worry if they're not completely submerged in the butter. As they cook, the morels will release liquid (making the sauce wonderfully mushroomy). The amount of sauce will increase and they will shrink. Add the thyme and gently simmer, stirring occasionally, until the morels are soft and tender, about 20 minutes. Adjust the seasoning with salt and pepper. Discard the thyme sprig and serve immediately.

pan-roasted hen-of-the-woods

SERVES 4

I think that what makes hen-of-the-woods such a great mushroom to pan-roast is its distinctive shape, with clusters full of planes and arches. They're quite beautiful, and when you roast them, each surface traps butter and seasoning. Because each cluster is a slightly different size and shape, each browns and softens to its own degree—making every bite a little different.

1 pound hen-of-the-woods mushrooms, cleaned and stems trimmed

About 4 tablespoons extra virgin olive oil

Kosher salt and freshly ground black pepper

2 tablespoons unsalted butter

4 fresh thyme sprigs

1 fresh rosemary sprig, broken in half

Using your hands, gently break the mushrooms into pieces about the size of golf balls.

Heat a skim of oil, about 2 tablespoons, in a large skillet over medium heat. Add half of the mushrooms and season them with salt and pepper. Cook them until they begin to color, about 3 minutes. Turn them over and continue cooking until the other sides begin to color, 2 to 3 minutes more. Add half of the butter, thyme, and rosemary. Baste the mushrooms with the melting butter and herbs for 1 minute. Drain on paper towels. Wipe out the pan and cook the remaining mushrooms in the same fashion. Discard the herb stems, then serve warm.

fish and shellfish

fish, I am told over and over again, is hard to cook properly. Honestly, this baffles me because it's just not true. In fact, a lot of fish is easier to cook than poultry and meat. You just need to keep a few things in mind.

The tastiest fish is freshly caught. The closer to that ideal you can get, the better. Fish loses flavor and its texture begins to change very quickly once it's out of the water. By the time it arrives at the store, it's already days old (at best). Whole fish last longer than fillets, and meatier fish fillets like salmon, tuna, and cod last longer than more delicate varieties like sole, but either way it's best to cook fish the day you buy it.

If you can, buy a whole fish. If you want fillets, it's best to have the fishmonger cut them or do it yourself. When buying whole fish, look for clear (not cloudy) eyes, bright red gills, and shiny skin. All fish should have a firm texture and a fresh sea smell. If you are buying fillets, look for smooth, glistening, evenly colored flesh. Avoid hacked-up fillets and fillets that look dried out or discolored.

Fish cooks quickly. Most fillets can be pan-roasted or sautéed in fewer than 10 minutes (sole cooks in closer to 3 minutes), making fish a perfect choice for a weeknight dinner, though it can be a little trickier when you are cooking for guests. I cook most fish until it flakes easily. Striped bass, black bass, red snapper, sole, and cod are all good cooked until the heat penetrates, making the flesh opaque throughout. When a fillet is done, you'll find that if you put a finger on either side of the thickest part of the fish and squeeze, it will give, but only a little. Salmon and tuna, I cook less, usually leaving the center just warm but not yet "set."

If you're worried about overcooking and want a little wiggle room, pick a method that is forgiving. Rather than pan-roasting, consider oil-poaching (see Olive Oil–Poached Salmon, page 174) or roast a whole fish—whole fish dry out much less abruptly than fillets (see Roasted Red Snapper with Potatoes and Onions, page 168). Although roasting a fish whole may seem daunting until you've done it a few times, it is a great, easy, forgiving way to go.

baccalà mantecato

MAKES ABOUT 2 CUPS

Like most Italians, my family celebrates Christmas Eve with a feast of fishes. The selection varies a little, but we always have baccalà mantecato, salt cod whipped with potato and oil and served as a rich, salty topping on toasted bread. The baccalà is made ahead, which is great when you're preparing a big meal. The problem is when to begin. The fish has to be soaked to remove excess salt. But no two pieces are the same, so you can't predict exactly how long it will take. I start 48 hours before I want to cook the fish. I cover it in water overnight, then change the water once or twice over the course of the following day. I pinch off a little and taste it. I want it nicely seasoned, not salty. If it's there, I go ahead and cook it; if not, I continue soaking it until it is. Once made, baccalà mantecato will keep beautifully for a week. One other thing: The potato and poached cod should both be warm when they go into the processor; otherwise the puree turns to glue.

½ pound salt cod fillet, cut into large pieces

1 medium Yukon Gold potato

Kosher salt and freshly ground black pepper

About ¾ cup extra virgin olive oil plus additional for serving

½ celery stalk, cut in half on the bias

½ carrot, peeled and cut in half on the bias

½ medium onion, cut into quarters

3 small garlic cloves, peeled, 2 minced

1 bay leaf

1 small fresh thyme sprig

About 1 quart whole milk

Pinch of minced peperoncini or red pepper flakes

2½ teaspoons chopped fresh flat-leaf parsley

Grilled or toasted bread (optional)

Put the cod in a large bowl with water to cover by at least 2". Cover the bowl with plastic wrap. Soak the cod in the refrigerator for 24 to 48 hours, changing the water several times a day, until the fish is no longer aggressively salty tasting. Drain.

Place the potatoes in a medium pot. Cover with salted water and bring to a boil. Adjust the heat and simmer until tender, about 20 minutes. Let sit in the cooking water off the heat until you are ready to use them.

While the potato cooks, heat a generous skim of oil, about 3 tablespoons, in a medium skillet over medium-low heat. Add the celery, carrot, and onion. Crush the whole garlic clove and add it to the pan. Season with salt and pepper, cover, and cook, stirring occasionally, until the garlic is fragrant and the vegetables soften, about 10 minutes. Add the bay leaf and thyme.

Add the soaked cod and enough milk to cover it. Put a lid on the pan and simmer gently over medium-low heat until the cod flakes easily, about 10 minutes. Allow the cod to cool a little in the cooking liquid off the heat. While it is still warm, use a slotted spoon to retrieve the pieces of fish and put them in a food processor. Strain and reserve the milk.

(recipe continues)

Salt cod is sold at Italian markets, fish stores, and gourmet shops. Salt cod is also available by mail, and because it keeps forever, it's fine to buy it this way.

Cut the fish into several pieces to make it easier to handle, but don't cut it too small or it will be hard to retrieve from the braising liquid. Cut the vegetables into large pieces. They're just used for flavoring and will be easier to remove.

Don't worry about oversoaking the fish. You can always add salt. And keep in mind that once the fish has been soaked, it becomes perishable, so cook it as soon as you can. After it's cooked, the fish will keep for a week.

Peel the warm potato, cut into chunks, and add to the processor. Add 3 tablespoons of the strained braising liquid, about half of the minced garlic, and ¼ cup oil. Pulse to mix. Then, with the machine running, add oil in a steady stream until the puree is the consistency of thick mayonnaise. Season the puree with lots of pepper, the remaining garlic, peperoncini, and salt to taste. Mix in the parsley. Serve at room temperature on grilled or toasted bread drizzled with a little oil if desired.

clams casino

MAKES 36

Clams casino may have first been served in Italian-American restaurants, but they taste like great home cooking. We always make them for Christmas Eve, and I love them. A few tips: When you cut the bacon, make the pieces big enough to more than cover the stuffing. The bacon will shrink when it cooks, and you want it to flavor the bread crumbs. I like the bacon when it's crispy and chewy at the same time, so watch the clams when you put them under the broiler. Rotate the pan, and once you see the edges of the bacon begin to brown, expect the clams to be done in about a minute. Remove each one as it becomes ready. And always make more than you think you need. Clams casino are addictive—they go down easier than potato chips, and no matter how many you make, they'll all disappear.

3 dozen littleneck clams

¼ pound bacon slices

½ cup dry white wine

½ cup bread crumbs

¼ cup minced roasted peppers in oil (about 1½ peppers, see page 128), oil reserved

3 tablespoons finely chopped fresh flat-leaf parsley

Pinch of minced peperoncini or red pepper flakes

1½ teaspoons dried oregano, preferably Sicilian

1 garlic clove, peeled and grated

3 tablespoons freshly grated Parmigiano-Reggiano

2½ tablespoons fresh lemon juice

Kosher salt

Use a rasp to grate the garlic so it's really fine.

Put the clams in a large bowl or pot. Cover them with cold water and let them soak for at least 1 hour.

Cut the bacon into 36 pieces, each a little larger than a clam. Set aside.

Lift the clams out of the soaking water and put them in a large pot. Add the wine, cover, and cook over high heat until the clams open, about 5 minutes. Lift the clams out of the pot and into a bowl to cool. Strain the clam juice through a fine sieve and reserve. (If you don't have a fine-mesh strainer, you

Soaking the clams gives them a chance to expel the sand in their bellies, but if you still wind up with a little in the bottom of the pot, leave the dregs there when you pour off the cooking liquid.

(recipe continues)

can decant the clam juice into a glass measuring cup; let the sediment settle to the bottom and pour off the juice, leaving the dregs in the cup.)

Preheat the broiler. Combine the bread crumbs, peppers, parsley, peperoncini, oregano, garlic, and Parmigiano in a bowl and mix well. Add 2 tablespoons of the oil used to marinate the peppers, 2 tablespoons of the clam broth, and the lemon juice. Mix and season with salt. The filling should be tasty and moist enough to hold together, so have a bite and add more broth, lemon juice, or seasoning if needed.

Discard the top shell of each clam. Arrange the clams on a baking sheet, loosening each one from its shell before you put it down. Mound a little less than 1 teaspoon of bread crumb mixture onto each clam. Lightly press the bread crumbs in place, then top with a piece of bacon.

Cook the clams under the broiler until the bacon begins to firm and brown, about 5 minutes. Serve warm.

fried oysters with shaved fennel and aioli

There's nothing I find more annoying than a restaurant server or chef telling me how to go about eating a particular dish. If I need a lesson, the dish is clearly way too complicated. But I guess there are exceptions to every rule, and this is one of them. So here it goes: Eat this dish with your fingers, everything in one bite—the hot creamy oyster, the cold crisp fennel, the spicy aioli, and the brightly acidic lemon will all come together and be 10 times better than any of the individual components.

FOR THE AIOLI:

    1 egg yolk

    ½ cup plus 2 tablespoons extra virgin olive oil

    2½ tablespoons fresh lemon juice

    1 small garlic clove, peeled

    Small pinch of peperoncini or red pepper flakes

    Kosher salt and freshly ground black pepper

FOR THE FENNEL:

    1 small fennel bulb

    1 lemon

FOR THE OYSTERS AND LEMON CONFIT GARNISH:

    ¼ cup all-purpose flour

    ¼ cup cornmeal

    Kosher salt

    Olive oil for frying

    24 medium oysters, shucked, bottom shells reserved and wiped clean

    9 slices Lemon Confit (page 257), quartered

*Aioli is garlic-flavored Maionese (page 256), and the same rules apply to making both sauces. **Most important:** Don't add the oil too quickly, particularly at the beginning. You are going to wind up with leftover aioli—this recipe makes a little over ½ cup, more than you need, but it's hard to make less. Use the rest on sandwiches or as a sauce for meat, fish, or vegetables.*

Use whatever type of oysters you prefer for this, although I would say that medium to large work best.

If you don't have lemon confit, a good squeeze of fresh lemon juice will suffice.

(recipe continues)

TO MAKE THE AIOLI: Whisk the egg yolk in a small bowl. Add the oil slowly, gradually dribbling it in while whisking continuously.

When the aioli begins to look about as thick as pancake batter and you have added about ½ cup of the oil, whisk in half of the lemon juice. Finely grate the garlic into the aioli and season with the peperoncini and a little salt and pepper.

Use a rasp to grate the garlic very finely.

Continue to incorporate the rest of the oil gradually. Adjust the seasoning with salt, pepper, and additional lemon juice. Refrigerate until ready to use. (Aioli will keep in the refrigerator for about a week.)

TO PREPARE THE FENNEL: Discard any discolored outer layers and then cut the fennel bulb into quarters lengthwise. Remove the core from each quarter. Shave the fennel as thinly as possible (this is most easily done with a mandolin). Put the fennel in a bowl, squeeze the lemon over the fennel, and toss together; reserve.

TO PREPARE THE OYSTERS AND GARNISH: Mix the flour and cornmeal and season with a little salt. Heat about ¼" oil in a deep skillet over medium-high heat. Working in batches, dredge the oysters in the flour mixture, then fry them until they are golden and crisp, about 20 seconds per side. Drain them on paper towels and salt each batch while still hot from the pan.

To assemble the dish, arrange the oyster shells on a serving plate. Mound shaved fennel in each shell. Spoon a little aioli onto the fennel and then top with a fried oyster. Finish with a piece of lemon confit and serve.

pickled sardines with vegetables

SERVES 6

In this recipe, inspired by some amazing pickled anchovies I had in Tuscany, you "cook" small fillets of fish in an acidic marinade (I use sardines, but fresh anchovies, mackerel, or any other full-flavored oily fish works). The size, thickness, and density of the fish determine the length of the cure. Big sardines need about 35 minutes, and small ones 10 to 15 minutes. They're ready when they are firm and opaque and no longer seem raw. Once they're done, pour off the pickling liquid or the fish will become too vinegary and ultimately break down. Cover the sardines with olive oil and they will keep for 3 or 4 days.

9 medium sardines (5 to 7 ounces each), filleted

Kosher salt and freshly ground black pepper

1 small fennel bulb, cored and cut into batons (about 2½" × ¼")

1 small yellow onion, peeled and thinly sliced

1 small carrot, peeled and thinly sliced

2 celery stalks, thinly sliced

¼ cup fresh flat-leaf parsley leaves

2 teaspoons dried oregano, preferably Sicilian

2 cups white or red wine vinegar

½ cup water

Fruity extra virgin olive oil

You'll notice that the aromatic vegetables here—fennel, onion, carrot, and celery—are the same I use to make soffritto. In this recipe, I use them raw to flavor the fish as it marinates and pickles. A nice thing to do is mince a little of each vegetable and use this uncooked soffritto—soffritto crudo—to garnish the sardines.

Sprinkle the sardines on both sides with salt and arrange them on a platter in a single layer. Let them cure at room temperature for 15 minutes.

Combine half of the fennel, onion, carrot, and celery in a baking dish large enough to hold the sardines in a single layer. Mix well. Sprinkle the vegetables with half of the parsley and oregano; season with salt and pepper.

Arrange the sardines, skin side up, over the vegetables (they should not overlap). Mix the remaining fennel, onion, carrot, and celery together. Distribute the vegetables evenly over the sardines, sprinkle with the remaining parsley and oregano, and season with salt and pepper. Pour the vinegar and water over the sardines. Allow the sardines to pickle at room temperature until they are opaque and slightly firm, about 25 minutes.

Pour off the pickling liquid. Really let it drain, then blot the fish dry with paper towels. Pour enough oil over the sardines and vegetables to cover them, then refrigerate until ready to serve. Serve the lightly pickled vegetables and sardines at room temperature or slightly chilled.

I think of the sardine recipe as a modern quick pickle, because I'm more interested in the flavor benefits than the preservative qualities of the marinade. The flavored vinegar draws out the moisture, essentially "cooking" the fillets—but I let them marinate only a short while because I don't want to lose the texture and overwhelm the taste of the fish. I get a little shelf life extension, but mostly I get great flavor.

pan-roasted sea scallops with white wine, capers, and lemon

SERVES 4 AS AN APPETIZER

Rule 1: Buy only "dry" scallops. When it comes to cooking, there are few absolutes, but "dry scallops or no scallops" is an unbreakable rule. "Wet" scallops are soaked in a chemical solution that plumps and whitens them and extends their shelf life. They contain so many chemicals and water that they will never brown properly and always wind up a tasteless mess.

Rule 2: Be prepared. Start to finish, the whole dish is going to take 7 minutes, but you need to be on your game the whole time. Everything has to be within arm's reach. If the phone rings, let it; otherwise, the scallops will overcook and be chewy.

Rule 3: Get your pan hot. Don't season the scallops until your pan is really blazing, and once they are in the pan, don't move them. Let a golden crust form on the bottom of each one. The scallops will then release from the pan and be easy to flip and finish cooking. I've added a simple pan sauce here, but salt and a squeeze of lemon is just as good.

Look for shiny off-white scallops that are not unnaturally plump. Check that the bottom of the container holding the scallops is more or less dry. They should feel a little sticky, not wet.

Make sure your skillet is not warped or bent or the scallops won't cook evenly.

FOR THE SCALLOPS:

About 2½ tablespoons extra virgin olive oil

8 medium to large sea scallops (U-10s if possible)

Kosher salt and freshly ground black pepper

1 tablespoon unsalted butter

FOR THE SAUCE:

2 tablespoons finely chopped shallot

½ teaspoon minced garlic

2½ tablespoons small capers

Juice of ½ lemon

¼ cup dry white wine

3 tablespoons chilled unsalted butter

2 tablespoons finely chopped fresh flat-leaf parsley

Kosher salt and freshly ground black pepper

TO MAKE THE SCALLOPS: Heat a medium skillet over high heat. When the pan is hot, add enough oil to cover the bottom, about 2½ tablespoons, and swirl it to make sure it spreads evenly. Wait until the oil begins to smoke, then season the scallops with salt and pepper and place them in the skillet, making sure to leave plenty of space between them.

Let the scallops cook undisturbed until a crust forms on the bottom and you begin to see color creeping up the edges, about 2½ minutes.

Flip each scallop, lower the heat slightly, and add the butter to the pan. Gather the scallops in the side of the pan opposite the handle. Tilt the pan slightly so the butter pools at the other end. Baste the scallops with the melting butter, continuing to cook until the scallops are just barely firm, about 1½ minutes more. Transfer the scallops to a plate while you make the sauce.

TO MAKE THE SAUCE: Pour the excess butter out of the pan, leaving just a skim. Adjust the heat to medium and add the shallot. Cook, moving them in the pan, until they begin to soften, a minute or so. Add the garlic and cook another minute, shaking the pan so the shallot and garlic won't stick or burn. (Note: If your pan starts to smoke when you add the shallot, lift it off the heat and shake it until it cools a little.)

Add the capers, lemon juice, and wine. Simmer vigorously until the pan is almost but not quite dry, about 2 minutes. Add any juices that have accumulated under the resting scallops. Make sure there are a couple of tablespoons of liquid in the pan (add a little water if the pan is dry). Finish the sauce by swirling in the butter, 1 tablespoon at a time. Add the parsley to the sauce and adjust the seasoning with salt and pepper. Reduce the heat to low and cook gently until the flavors blend, another minute or so. Transfer the scallops to warm plates. Spoon the sauce over them and serve.

The amount of time it will take for a crust to form will vary depending on the sugar content of your scallops. You can peek, lifting an edge with a spatula or fork, to see if the scallop is nicely browned.

the art of pan sauces

Once you learn the process of making a pan sauce like this one, you can substitute any fish you like. You can also start to play around with substituting ingredients in the sauce—instead of capers, try some black or green olives; instead of lemon juice, use another citrus; instead of parsley, try mint, tarragon, or thyme. Get comfortable with the process and you can put your own signature on the foods that you make.

red-wine braised octopus

SERVES 4 TO 6

Cooking octopus at home is not everyone's cup of tea. But if you feel like taking it on, this is really tasty. And cooked my way, the octopus is tender in an hour. I use a covered pot and weight the lid so all of the aromatic steam stays inside. I wind up with something like a homemade pressure cooker. It works.

It is okay to use frozen octopus for this recipe. Freezing tenderizes the flesh without compromising the flavor.

2 octopus (about 1 pound each)
¼ cup extra virgin olive oil
3 garlic cloves, peeled and crushed
2 dried peperoncini
About 2 cups dry red wine

The outer purple layer of an octopus is gelatinous when warm. If you pull it off (suckers and all), you are left with white meat that looks like calamari. This is what I do when I want to make a seafood salad. But when I plan to serve whole legs hot, I keep that outer layer—I love the color and the texture contrast between the firm/tender inside and the slightly gooey, gelatinous outside.

Clean each octopus by rubbing it against the inside of a colander under running water. (Grit gets lodged in the suckers, and rubbing the legs against the uneven surface dislodges it.) Dry the octopus and cut it right below the eyes. Remove the beak. Then cut the head again just above the eyes and discard them. Rinse out the innards and pull the membrane from the head. Set the head aside. Divide the legs into two portions (you will wind up with a cleaned head and two groups of four legs per octopus).

Put the oil, garlic, and peperoncini in a pot that has a tight-fitting lid—but don't put the lid on yet; cook over low heat.

When the garlic becomes fragrant and begins to color, raise the heat to medium-high. One at a time, hold each piece of octopus with tongs and sear it in the oil. Move the octopus across the bottom of the pan through the oil just until it begins to plump, turning a beautiful deep color, and the tentacles curl (but not so long that the octopus begins to release liquid), about 2 minutes. Put the cooked octopus in a bowl.

When all of the octopus has been seared, return the pieces to the pot in a single layer (follow the natural coil of the legs as you arrange them in the pot). Add enough wine to come halfway up the octopus. Cover the pot, then weight the lid with an overturned pot and heavy cans. Reduce the heat to low and simmer the octopus until it is tender, 1 hour.

Using a kitchen fork, stab each piece in the thickest place and carefully transfer it to a baking sheet. Reserve the braising liquid. (When the octopus is hot, you need to handle it carefully. The outer purple layer is gelatinous when warm and will pull off if roughly treated. I cool the octopus, portion it, and reheat it. But if you want to serve it immediately, be very gentle.)

Don't cool the octopus in the braising liquid. The liquid contains so much gelatin that it will solidify as it cools, making the octopus hard to remove. So store the octopus and liquid separately.

Once the octopus is cool, you can separate the tentacles and easily cut the head into several pieces. Shortly before serving, preheat the oven to 375°F. Arrange the octopus pieces in a shallow flameproof roasting pan in a single layer. Add enough of the reserved braising liquid to come halfway up the octopus; bring it to a boil on the stove and then put it in the oven. Baste the octopus with the sauce frequently while it heats through, about 15 minutes. It will be beautifully glazed. Serve warm or at room temperature.

roasted red snapper
with potatoes and onions

SERVES 4

When I first started cooking, one of the best cooks on the planet, my aunt (zia) Leda, asked me to make her dinner. We were at her home in upstate New York. She kept the most amazing vegetable and herb gardens there, always harvesting more produce than she knew what to do with. She pulled some fresh potatoes and onions from the dirt and clipped a bunch of herbs. She handed it all over to me with a beautiful red snapper, and I set to work. I tossed the potatoes with the onions and rosemary and got them started in the oven. I seasoned the fish, then fanned out the belly and the collarbones so it would stand straight up (I thought it looked like a fish swimming). Then I roasted it on the potatoes. Because the fish wasn't on its side, the heat of the oven circulated evenly all around it. Zia Leda still talks about how beautiful and how delicious it was.

2 small red onions, peeled and thinly sliced

2 medium Yukon Gold potatoes, peeled, halved, and thinly sliced

2 garlic cloves, peeled and thinly sliced

1 tablespoon chopped fresh rosemary plus 2 small branches

1 lemon, halved and sliced thinly, plus lemon wedges for garnish

6 tablespoons extra virgin olive oil plus additional for serving

Kosher salt and freshly ground black pepper

1 red snapper (3 pounds), gutted and scaled

Sea salt for garnish

Be careful when you handle whole fish. The fins can be very sharp, so trim them—carefully.

Getting the pan hot on the oven floor first helps the potatoes brown. If this doesn't work in your oven, just make sure to let the pan get really hot.

Preheat the oven to 375°F. Put a baking sheet in the oven to heat. I put mine directly on the oven floor.

Combine the onions, potatoes, garlic, chopped rosemary, and all but 6 of the lemon slices in a large bowl. Add 4 tablespoons oil, season generously with salt and pepper, and mix well.

Carefully remove the baking sheet from the oven. Spread the potato mixture in a single layer on the sheet and return it to the oven floor for 10 minutes.

While the pan heats, rinse and dry the fish, inside and out. Make three deep, angled slits—all the way to, but not through, the bones on each side of the body. Season the fish inside and out with salt and pepper. Snap off 6 small

sprigs from the rosemary branches and stick a sprig in each slit, along with a slice of lemon. Rub or brush the fish with the remaining 2 tablespoons oil.

Take the pan out of the oven, then spreading the sides of the stomach cavity apart, stand the fish on the potatoes, on its belly. Return the pan to the oven, this time placing it on a rack in the center. Increase the heat to 425°F and roast until the fish is opaque and flakes easily and the potatoes are golden, about 30 minutes. Remove the fish from the oven and allow it to rest for 10 minutes. Serve garnished with lemon wedges, sea salt, and oil if desired.

This method works very well for a wide variety of meaty midsized fish such as sea bass, small striped bass, and branzini. The cooking time will depend on the size and density of the fish.

striped bass al cartoccio

SERVES 4

This is a flavorful, healthy way to cook fish. The basic formula is to create a packet for the fish out of parchment (aluminum foil also works), then add flavorings like herbs, shallots, olives, and a little bit of lemon juice and olive oil. Seal and bake the fish in the packet, and the fish winds up perfectly steamed. When you pull the package open, it's so aromatic that I like to bring the fish in the parchment to the table and serve it there so everyone gets to enjoy the wonderful smell and anticipate the taste. You can wrap and steam each serving individually, or steam all the fish in one packet, but either way, I suggest you cut the fillets into portions first to make serving it easier.

3 tablespoons extra virgin olive oil

Kosher salt and freshly ground black pepper

8 fresh rosemary sprigs

1 lemon, thinly sliced

1 skinless striped bass fillet (2 pounds), about ½" thick,
    cut into four 8-ounce pieces

¼ cup Niçoise olives, pitted if desired

2 large shallots, peeled and sliced as thinly as possible

2 tablespoons finely chopped fresh flat-leaf parsley

When I cook striped bass or other fish with thick skin, I remove it. Thin-skinned fish like black bass can be cooked with the skin on.

A few flavoring additions worth considering: white or red wine or vermouth; garlic; tarragon; thyme; basil; spices like coriander, mustard, or bay. Or try adding artichokes, potatoes, mushrooms, truffles, tomatoes, leeks, fennel, or celery. Just remember to cut vegetables small enough to cook quickly, and precook veggies (like artichokes and potatoes) that need more time than the fish will take to cook.

Preheat the oven to 400°F. Place a baking sheet in the oven to heat.

Meanwhile, cut 4 large pieces (16" x 12½") of parchment and place them on a clean work surface. Fold the parchment piece in half, then cut each in a half oval. Unfold the parchment, brush each piece with a little oil, then sprinkle with salt and pepper. Lay 2 sprigs of rosemary and a few lemon slices on each piece. Top with a portion of fish. Season the fish with salt and pepper and then put the remaining lemon slices on top. Scatter the olives over the fish. Separate the sliced shallots into rings and put them on the fish as well. Drizzle the remaining oil over all, then sprinkle with the parsley.

Seal the fish in the pouches—you want to fold one half over the other then gather the two sides together and fold and crimp the edges tightly enough to seal—think Jiffy Pop. Put the packet on the preheated baking sheet and steam

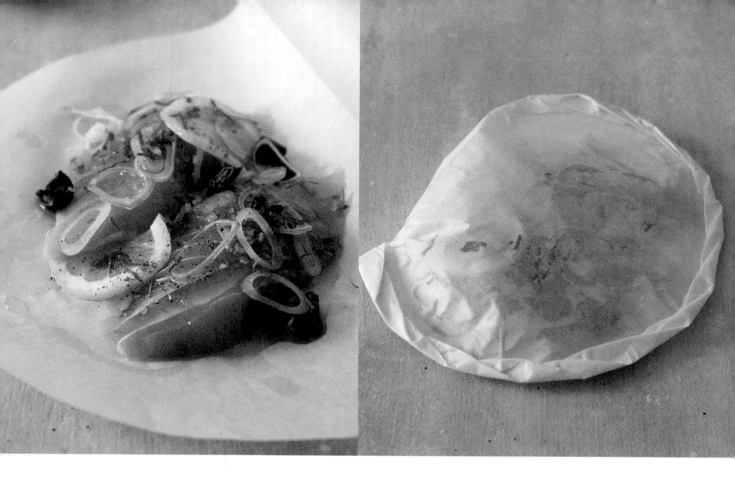

the fish in the oven until it is tender, about 15 minutes. (You can check by giving the fish in the foil a squeeze; if it gives easily, then it's done. If you're not sure, it's okay to peek; just open the packet up as little as possible and close it up quickly if the fish isn't ready.)

Virtually any fish can be cooked this way, with only slight alterations in the method. The trick is that because the fish is enclosed in parchment, it can be hard to tell when it is done, the time ranging from less than 5 minutes to as much as 30. Really delicate fillets like sole and flounder will cook the most quickly, the exact time depending on the size of the fillet. With larger, denser fish, I cut thick fillets on the bias into medallions as this reduces the cooking time. It also increases the surface area, so flavorings have more impact on the finished dish.

roasted salmon with roasted pepper salad

SERVES 4

This cooking method—and in fact this whole recipe—works with a wide variety of fish. Try skin-on fillets of cod, black bass, striped bass, or snapper. If you are using larger, thicker fillets, cook the skin side at a slightly lower temperature for a longer time to make sure the fish gets cooked through. Be particularly careful when you're cooking skin-on fillets of wild striped bass. Because the skin is thick, it takes a surprisingly long time for the heat to begin to move up into the meat and cook it.

FOR THE SALMON:

> 4 skin-on salmon fillets (6 ounces each)
>
> About 1 tablespoon extra virgin olive oil
>
> Kosher salt and freshly ground black pepper

FOR THE PEPPER SALAD:

> 1 cup julienned roasted peppers (½ recipe page 128) plus 2 tablespoons of marinade
>
> 2 tablespoons drained capers
>
> Grated zest and juice of 1 lemon
>
> ¼ cup fresh flat-leaf parsley leaves
>
> Kosher salt and freshly ground black pepper

TO MAKE THE SALMON: Scrape the skin of each fillet with a knife, then dry well with paper towels. Place the fillets on a plate skin side up and refrigerate uncovered for about
1 hour.

Shortly before you are ready to serve, heat a large skillet over high heat. Add enough oil to skim the surface, about 1 tablespoon. Season the salmon on both sides with salt and pepper and put the fillets in the pan skin side down. (Be sure not to crowd the pan; you want at least ½" of space around each fillet. If your pan isn't big enough, use two pans or work in batches.) After about a minute or two, reduce the heat to medium-high and cook the salmon until the skin begins to brown, about 5 minutes. Shake the pan to loosen the fish. If the fish slides easily, continue cooking until the skin is crispy, about 1 minute more. If the fish is sticking, lower the heat and continue cooking until the skin loosens, 1½ to 3 minutes. Flip the fillets and cook them until they feel slightly firm when squeezed gently, about 2 minutes.

TO MAKE THE PEPPER SALAD: While the fish cooks, combine the peppers, capers, lemon zest, and parsley in a bowl. Dress the salad with the reserved marinade and lemon juice and season it with salt and pepper. Mix well.

Transfer the salmon to warm plates. Spoon pepper salad over each fillet and serve.

Adding the fish cools the pan. Wait a few minutes until it comes back up to temperature, then reduce the heat so the skin can cook gradually and the heat has time to penetrate the fish.

olive oil–poached salmon

SERVES 4

This technique is used a fair amount in restaurants these days, and I think it works just as well at home. The fish fillet is literally poached in herb and garlic–infused olive oil, sealing in the natural juices without penetrating so the fish winds up moist and not at all greasy. The oil temperature is kept low, so it's a very forgiving method of cooking—a few minutes extra aren't a problem. The tricky thing is controlling the heat. Keep your flame on low, but watch it. The best gauge is a thermometer (the oil should never creep above 180°F), but lacking that, keep an eye on the oil—you don't want more than a few tiny bubbles rising to the surface. Meaty, firm-fleshed fish like halibut, striped bass, black bass, or red snapper can be cooked this way.

My first preference when I am going to cook salmon is wild fish. Recently, there have been great strides made in farming salmon—there are some really good farms producing high-quality fish in a thoughtful way. Ask your fishmonger about the source, but if he can't tell you, beware.

Play around with herbs and spices used to flavor the oil. I like fresh ginger, lemongrass, virtually any fresh herb, citrus peels of all kinds, toasted coriander seeds, cardamom, and hot pepper.

Take your time and work over low heat. No harm will come from going too slowly.

10 fresh thyme sprigs

1 large fresh rosemary sprig

2 garlic cloves, peeled and lightly crushed

Strips of peel from 1 lemon, white pith removed

About 3 cups olive oil

2 pounds salmon fillet, cut into 4 pieces and brought to room temperature

Kosher salt and freshly ground black pepper

Combine the thyme, rosemary, garlic, lemon peel, and oil in a high-sided skillet just large enough to hold the salmon pieces in a single layer without touching. Heat the oil over medium-low, reducing the heat when it reaches 180°F and small bubbles begin to appear.

Season the fish on both sides with salt and pepper and add the fillets to the oil, making sure there is a little room between them. If the oil doesn't cover the salmon, add a little more. The oil temperature will drop when you add the fish, especially if it comes straight from the refrigerator. Cook the salmon until it is pale pink on top and flakes easily, about 13 minutes, watching the oil temperature carefully. Remove the fillets from the oil, drain on a plate lined with paper towels, and serve.

skate with pomegranate vinaigrette

SERVES 4

This is not something I grew up eating, but somehow the fresh taste of sautéed fish with a nicely acidic vinaigrette strikes me the same way—simple, straightforward cooking of really tasty food. Skate is a delicious fish, firmer and more flavorful than sole and more delicate than cod, but substitute what you like. I begin my vinaigrette with pomegranate juice; it's nice and tart and the color is beautiful, but again, feel free to substitute. Any acidic fruit juice will work—grapefruit, lime, or orange, alone or in combination.

FOR THE VINAIGRETTE:

Although with citrus I always juice the fruit myself, I think bottled pomegranate juice is fine.

¼ cup pomegranate juice

1 tablespoon finely minced shallot

Kosher salt and freshly ground black pepper

½ cup grape seed oil

¼ cup extra virgin olive oil

Fresh lemon juice

By combining neutral-tasting grape seed oil and heavier, more assertive olive oil, you wind up with a clean-tasting sauce with a hint of olive.

FOR THE FISH:

2 pounds boneless skate fillets

Kosher salt and freshly ground black pepper

1 cup all-purpose flour

Olive oil for frying

1½ tablespoons chopped fresh flat-leaf parsley

Add a squeeze of lemon if you like a vinaigrette with bite.

TO MAKE THE VINAIGRETTE: Combine the pomegranate juice and shallot in a bowl. Season with salt and pepper. While whisking continuously, gradually add the grape seed and olive oils. Adjust the seasoning with lemon juice, salt, and pepper and set aside.

TO MAKE THE FISH: If the skate wings are large, cut them in half so they are easier to manage in the pan. Season the skate with salt and pepper.

Place the flour on a plate and season it with salt and pepper. Heat about ⅛" oil in a large skillet over medium heat.

Working in batches, dredge the fish in the flour and shake off the excess. Increase the heat to medium-high and add a few pieces of fish to the pan, taking care not to crowd the pan.

Cook the fish until it is crisp and golden, about 2 minutes, then turn it over and cook until the second side is golden and the fish flaky, 1 to 2 minutes more. Transfer the cooked fish to a plate lined with paper towels to drain.

To serve, put the fish on warm plates and spoon the vinaigrette over the fish. Garnish with parsley and serve.

This vinaigrette has a tendency to separate. Don't worry. Just give it a good whisk right before you serve it (or keep it in a jar and give it a vigorous shake before you use it).

a handy tool

I use the same setup for both steaming and smoking: a deep metal pan with a shallow perforated metal insert and a lid. Somewhere along the way, I figured out that these components, manufactured for professional food storage, are great to cook in.

What you want is a 6-inch-deep half hotel pan, a 2-inch-deep perforated half hotel pan, and a half-pan lid. These pieces are easiest to find at restaurant supply stores, or you can order them by mail.

To steam, simply put water in the bottom and place the food to be steamed in the insert. Cover and cook over high heat. Sometimes I add aromatics, flavoring the liquid (and therefore the steam). Try adding leeks, onions, carrot, celery, and wine to the water to create a court-bouillon. You can also line the insert with herbs, lemons, or other aromatics. I steam fish (whole and fillets), vegetables, and poultry this way.

Smoking is not much harder. Soak 3 cups of wood chips (whatever kind you prefer) in water for at least an hour. Drain the chips and put them in the bottom of the hotel pan; top with the insert. Put the food in the insert, cover, and put the pan on the burner over high heat. The metal pan will heat and cause the wet wood chips to smoke. Your kitchen will get smoky, so be prepared—or put the smoker right on a very hot grill outdoors.

I like to smoke salmon and sturgeon (line the insert with lemon slices and herbs to subtly flavor the fish and prevent it from sticking). But I also do chickpeas, onions, and garlic. I smoke the chickpeas after I soak them but before I cook them. I slice the onions and peel the garlic. The onions and garlic are a great place to begin a homemade barbecue sauce or a soup, adding an earthy depth of flavor. Add smoked onions to pureed lentil or pea soup and people will swear you added bacon. Just remember, smoke is a strong flavor, so don't overdo it. Start slowly and, when you think you have gotten it just right, make a note so you can remember the timing.

steamed black bass with olive oil and lemon

SERVES 4

This is a method to add to your repertoire and vary to suit your situation and taste. Although I wouldn't cook swordfish or tuna this way, steaming works beautifully with almost every other kind of fish. I steam in a square metal pan with a perforated insert meant for storing food. A Chinese bamboo steamer works well too. Steamed fish is delicious with a drizzle of good olive oil, a little lemon, and some sea salt, but experiment. My only other piece of advice: The fish has to be really fresh. Such a simple treatment flatters perfection but reveals all flaws.

4 black bass fillets (5 to 6 ounces each)

Kosher salt and freshly ground black pepper

About 1½ tablespoons extra virgin olive oil plus additional for serving

2 lemons, sliced

5 fresh thyme sprigs

Sea salt

1 lemon, cut into quarters

Season the fillets on both sides with salt and pepper, then brush them with oil.

Line the bottom of the insert with the lemon and thyme. Arrange the fillets skin side up on the lemon slices. Add about 3" of boiling water to the steamer pan and bring it back to a boil over high heat. Fit the insert into the steamer, cover it tightly, and steam the fish until it is cooked through and flakes easily, about 5 minutes. Serve sprinkled with sea salt and drizzled with lemon juice and oil.

You might consider a sauce with this. A vinaigrette would work well. Take a look at the recipe for Skate with Pomegranate Vinaigrette (page 176) for ideas. A spring pea puree or another vegetable puree would also make a nice sauce; see page 77 for more on this.

Adjust the cooking time depending on the thickness of the fillets and the delicacy of the fish. Check thin, delicate fish after about 3 minutes, medium-flake fish like black bass after 5 minutes, and meatier fish after about 7 minutes.

fried fillet of sole

SERVES 4

I look for sole or flounder fillets that are really thin—they cook more quickly and more evenly, and you get the right proportion of crust to flaky fish. Cutting them down to manageable size, 4" to 6", makes them easier to handle in the pan. Notice I don't use bread crumbs. I flour the fillets and then dip them in egg. Bread crumbs would overpower the delicate texture of the fish. A squeeze of lemon, a little salt, and a sprinkle of parsley and you are good to go.

2 pounds sole or flounder fillets

About 1 cup all-purpose flour

Kosher salt and freshly ground black pepper

4 eggs

Olive oil for frying

1 lemon, cut into wedges for garnish

1½ tablespoons chopped fresh flat-leaf parsley

It is fine to use a blend of olive and vegetable oils for frying.

Cut the fillets into pieces 4" to 6" long.

Place the flour on a plate and season it with salt and pepper. Crack the eggs into a wide shallow bowl and beat them lightly.

Heat about ¼" oil in a large skillet over medium heat.

Leftover fried fish is great at room temperature or even cold from the refrigerator. Try it in a sandwich with caper mayonnaise and lettuce or as is, simply dressed with lemon juice and a little olive oil.

Working in batches, dredge the fish in the flour, shake off the excess, and dip the fillets into the egg. Increase the heat to medium-high and add a few pieces of fish to the pan, making sure not to crowd the pan.

Cook the fish until it is crisp and golden, about 2 minutes. Turn it over and cook until the second side is also golden and the fish is flaky, 1 to 2 minutes more. Transfer the fish to a plate lined with paper towels to drain. Sprinkle with salt and serve with lemon wedges and a little chopped parsley.

calamari salad with chickpeas, celery, and olives

SERVES 4 TO 6

The thing about squid is that you must cook it very quickly or very slowly, or it winds up rubbery. In this recipe, I handle the squid gently. I start off poaching it, bringing the water just short of a simmer, then pull the pot off the heat to finish cooking the squid in the residual heat. Take the pot off the stove when the first bubbles begin to appear, then relax; it's not going to overcook.

1½ pounds fresh-cleaned squid bodies and tentacles

Kosher salt

½ cup pitted Niçoise olives

¾ cup extra virgin olive oil

1 garlic clove, peeled

¾ cup thinly sliced celery hearts and chopped leaves

Pinch of minced peperoncini

1 teaspoon dried Sicilian oregano

1½ cups cooked chickpeas (see variation to Cannellini Beans Stewed with Sage on page 117)

¼ cup finely chopped fresh flat-leaf parsley

Juice of 1 lemon or to taste

This salad is also very good made with grilled squid marinated in about 2 tablespoons of olive oil and salt and pepper. Slice the grilled squid bodies into rings and add them to the bowl, then proceed as described in the recipe.

Another way to jazz things up is to smoke the chickpeas. On page 178, you'll find a picture of the contraption I use for smoking and everything you'll need to know.

Slice the squid bodies into rings about ¼" thick. Leave the tentacles whole or divide them in half if they are big. Put the squid in a medium pot; add water to cover and a generous amount of salt. Heat the water over medium-high heat just until the first bubbles appear—do not let the water boil. Remove the pot from the stove and let stand, uncovered, until the squid is opaque, 10 to 15 minutes.

Chop the olives and put them in a large bowl. Add the oil. Grate the garlic into the oil, then add the celery, peperoncini, oregano, and chickpeas. Mix well.

Drain the squid and blot dry on paper towels. Add the warm squid to the oil mixture. Add the parsley and lemon juice and salt to taste. Mix well and serve at room temperature.

cacciucco (seafood stew)

SERVES 6

Cacciucco, a seafood stew my mother grew up eating during summer visits to the beach in Viareggio, has a wonderful distinctive flavor, at the same time both sweet and briny. The secret is gently stewing calamari with tomato and wine. Calamari is mostly water—think about how much it shrinks when it cooks—so when all that liquid goes into the broth, it gives it a great sea flavor, quite different from fish stock.

½ cup extra virgin olive oil

1 cup minced fennel

1 cup minced celery

2 cups minced onions

1 tablespoon dried oregano, preferably Sicilian

Pinch of minced peperoncini or red pepper flakes

Kosher salt and freshly ground black pepper

1½ pounds cleaned squid (about 2 pounds uncleaned), bodies sliced into ½" rounds and tentacles halved if very large

2 cups dry white wine

5 cups tomato puree (Pomarola, page 18, or canned)

Peel of 1 lemon (in large pieces; pith removed)

12 little neck clams, soaked in cold water for 1 hour

18 mussels, scrubbed and beards removed (this is easiest if you use a towel to grip)

12 shrimp, peeled and deveined

About ¾ pound firm white fish fillet, cut into 12 pieces

3 tablespoons finely minced flat-leaf parsley

Finely grated zest of 2 lemons

12 Crostini (page 189), rubbed with garlic

If you have Blond Soffritto Base (page 12), heat 2 cups, season with oregano and peperoncini, and fry until fragrant. Reduce the heat, add the squid, and proceed as directed.

If you want a more decadent dish, you can include lobster tails and claws in the cacciucco. Parboil the claws for 7 minutes and the tail for 5 minutes. Remove the meat from the shell and add it to the cacciucco 2 minutes or so after you add the fish.

You can prepare the soffritto and the base in advance, but the third stage, adding the fish and shellfish, has to happen when people are ready to eat.

Heat the oil in a large pot over medium-high heat. Add the minced vegetables and fry, stirring frequently. When the vegetables begin to soften, add the oregano, peperoncini, and salt and pepper to taste. Fry the soffritto, stirring frequently, until the vegetables are a pale golden color, about 15 minutes.

Reduce the heat to medium-low and add the squid. Mix well and cook, stirring occasionally, until the squid releases its liquid, becomes firm and opaque, and shrinks considerably, 15 to 20 minutes. (You'll notice that when you add the squid, it will release lots of liquid, then gradually the liquid will evaporate and concentrate. When you see the soffritto vegetables and squid frying in the oil, it's time to add the wine.)

Pour in the wine, increase the heat to medium-high, and simmer actively until the pan is almost dry again, about 20 minutes.

Add the tomato puree and lemon peel; season with salt and pepper. Reduce the heat and simmer gently, stirring occasionally, until the oil begins to separate from the tomato and rise to the surface, about 40 minutes. (The cacciucco base may be cooled and refrigerated or frozen at this point.)

Bring the cacciucco base to a gentle simmer. Adjust the seasoning with salt, pepper, and peperoncini. Remove and discard the lemon peel. Add the clams and let them cook for 3 minutes. Add the mussels, shrimp, and fish. Simmer until the shellfish open and the fish is firm and opaque, about 5 minutes.

While the cacciucco cooks, prepare the gremolata by chopping the parsley with the grated lemon zest. Ladle the cacciucco into warm bowls. Top with gremolata, season with sea salt, and serve with the crostini.

The base is really useful. Use it as is, spooning the calamari and braising liquid over the croutons or pasta. Finish with olive oil, parsley, and sea salt for a snack or light meal. Or strain the base and use the briny broth to braise monkfish tails, halibut, cod, snapper, or bass. I also cook mussels in the strained base to serve alone as a stew or over pasta.

*chicken and
other birds*

it's funny how food goes in and out of style. I read somewhere that at one time in Europe chicken was considered the height of luxurious dining, far more exotic than peacock. Flash-forward to the 1920s and chicken came to mind when the Republican Party wanted an approachable symbol of a prosperous, satisfied populace. Today, while there may not be a chicken in every pot, there are certainly plenty of chickens (and packages of their various parts) in every supermarket. Chicken has eclipsed "the other white meat," not to mention other fowl and fish. It's even challenging the reign supreme of red meat. There's lots of chicken and lots of chicken recipes out there—whole books, in fact, so I wanted to be particularly thoughtful about which recipes I passed along.

Sadly, the more popular chicken has become, the harder it is to find a chicken that tastes like chicken. Mass production has rendered most of the chicken we see plumper and perhaps more appealing looking but far less good to eat. What I've tried to do is gather recipes that, with a little art, make even today's bland, commercially produced birds taste delicious. I've also included recipes that make use of a technique, method, or procedure that's worth knowing about. In Chicken with Pancetta and Sage (page 193), for example, I wrap a chicken breast with pancetta, a technique that works just as well with other lean meat and meaty fish. I've also included a recipe for fried chicken the way my mother makes it, Tuscan Fried Chicken with Sage (page 190), simply because it's one of my favorite foods. All of the recipes in this section work with supermarket chicken but are even better with free-range, hormone-free, air-chilled birds, a worthwhile investment in taste and, I believe, your health.

I've also included one recipe for rabbit in this chapter, although technically it's not poultry. However, rabbit and chicken are interchangeable in many of these recipes, and it portions more like poultry than pork or lamb, so it seemed a better fit.

chicken liver crostini

MAKES ABOUT 20

This dish is a true Tuscan classic. The secret to getting the best flavor is browning, without overcooking, the chicken livers. Before they go into the pan, get them really dry and the pan really hot. Never salt them until just before cooking and cook the livers without moving them until they get a nice crust. You also want to caramelize the onions—their sweet flavor complements the richness of the livers.

Sautéed chicken livers are the starting point for a great sauce. Put the chopped browned livers and caramelized onions in a small saucepan and add enough chicken broth to just cover, about ½ cup. Add 1 tablespoon extra virgin olive oil and warm over low heat. Puree using a handheld immersion blender. If the sauce is too thick, mix in a little more broth or some water. Season with salt and pepper and serve with roasted chicken.

½ pound chicken livers

2 tablespoons unsalted butter

4 tablespoons extra virgin olive oil

1 cup finely chopped onion

Kosher salt and freshly ground black pepper

1 fresh sage sprig

1 fresh rosemary sprig

½ anchovy fillet, minced

½ tablespoon drained capers

¼ cup cognac or other deglazing liquid (see Notes)

1–2 baguettes, sliced, toasted, and seasoned with salt and pepper

Clean the livers, removing any veins, sinew, and fat. Lay them on towels to dry.

Heat the butter and 1 tablespoon oil in a large skillet over high heat. Add the onion and season with salt and pepper. Add the sage and rosemary and cook, stirring occasionally, until the onion starts to soften and color, about 5 minutes. Add the anchovy and capers, reduce the heat to medium-high, and continue cooking until the onion is soft and caramelized, about 10 minutes more. Transfer the onion to a bowl and wipe out the pan.

Pat the livers dry with a towel. Heat the skillet over high heat. Add the remaining 3 tablespoons oil. Season the livers with salt and pepper and immediately place them in the pan in a single well-spaced layer.

Cook the livers without disturbing them until they get nicely browned, about 2 minutes, then flip them over. Cook for 1 minute more, then add the onion. Mix to distribute the onion evenly. Stand back from the stove and carefully add the cognac (it will flame); cook until the flames burn out and the pan is more or less dry, about 30 seconds. Remove the pan from the heat.

I used cognac to deglaze here, but there are other options, including brandy, white or red wine, sherry, and Marsala.

Allow the livers to cool for 15 minutes. Remove and discard the herbs, then chop the livers finely or pulse the mixture in a food processor. Taste and adjust the seasoning if necessary with salt and pepper. Serve at room temperature on toasted baguette slices. The chicken liver mixture will keep in the refrigerator for about a week.

crostini

It's kind of silly to give a recipe for toasted bread—which is what crostini are. But here goes. Cut slices of country bread, French, Italian, sourdough—whatever you prefer—as thick as makes sense. If you're going to serve the crostini with a salad, for example, slice them paper thin. If you're going to top them with chicken liver spread (Chicken Liver Crostini) or whipped salt cod (Baccalà Mantecato, page 154), then slice them a little thicker. Heat your oven to 350°F. Coat a baking pan with extra virgin olive oil. Arrange the bread on the pan, then flip each slice over so you get some oil on both sides. Season the bread with salt and pepper and toast until golden and crunchy. The time will depend on the type of bread you are using and the thickness of your crostini. Use immediately or store in sealed plastic bags.

tuscan fried chicken with sage

SERVES 6 TO 8

As a kid, I always looked forward to family picnics, because I knew my mother would pack this fried chicken. Unlike southern-style fried chicken with its crunchy coating, this Tuscan version has the softer crust you get from a quick dip in flour and then beaten egg. I like it better and I like it best at room temperature when you can really appreciate the complementary textures and flavors.

I cut the chicken by taking off the wings and legs. Cut each breast into thirds and each thigh in half. If you prefer, buy the chicken pieces you like best; just remember to cut them down to size so the meat and crust cook in the same short time and you wind up with the right ratio of crisp skin to juicy meat.

It is not necessary to use extra virgin olive oil here. A blend of olive oil and a neutral-tasting vegetable oil will work.

When a batch of chicken is in the pan, the oil should come about half-way up the pieces. Add more oil if necessary.

Remember to adjust the heat to maintain an even temperature.

1 chicken, cut into 14 pieces (see Note)
¼ cup olive oil plus additional for frying
2 tablespoons finely chopped fresh sage
Kosher salt and freshly ground black pepper
About 2 cups all-purpose flour
5 eggs, lightly beaten

Combine the chicken, ¼ cup oil, and the sage in a bowl or plastic bag. Season the chicken liberally with salt and pepper. Mix to coat the pieces, then marinate at room temperature for about 20 minutes.

Heat ½" oil in a large high-sided skillet over medium heat. Working in batches, dredge the chicken in flour, starting with smaller pieces. Shake off the excess flour and then dip the chicken into the egg.

Carefully place just a few pieces of the egg-dipped chicken in the skillet, adding the chicken to the oil one piece at a time and allowing 30 seconds or so between additions. This will prevent the oil from cooling down. Adjust the heat so the oil looks shimmery and glistening, but not smoking or sputtering.

Fry the chicken until golden on one side, about 7 minutes. Turn and continue cooking until each piece is uniformly crisp and golden and the internal juices run clear, about 5 minutes more. Transfer the fried chicken to a plate lined with paper towels to drain and sprinkle with salt.

Repeat, dipping the remaining pieces of chicken in flour and egg and then frying. When you begin to fry larger pieces (the drumsticks), lower the heat a little and expect to cook each piece closer to 15 minutes in all. Let the chicken rest at room temperature for at least 5 minutes before serving.

grilled quail

SERVES 6

This is a great way to cook quail, a bird that is, in my opinion, underappreciated. It is a nice alternative to more expected cookout fare. At Hearth, we serve grilled quail year-round, varying the farro salad accompaniment to suit the season (see Winter Farro Salad, page 104, and Summer Farro Salad, page 105). Marinate the quail in the refrigerator overnight, but if you're pressed for time, 2 hours at room temperature will do.

Look for fresh or frozen quail that have been butterflied with all but leg bones removed. They are available at specialty food stores and can also be ordered by mail.

When you feel like splurging, try drizzling the quail with really good aged Modena balsamic just before you serve them.

12 semi-boneless quail

6 tablespoons extra virgin olive oil

3 tablespoons balsamic vinegar plus additional for serving

1 garlic clove, peeled and thinly sliced

Peel of ½ lemon, pith removed

1 fresh rosemary sprig plus additional for serving

2 fresh thyme sprigs plus additional for serving

Kosher salt and cracked black pepper

Combine the quail, oil, vinegar, garlic, lemon peel, rosemary, and thyme in a large plastic storage bag. Season the quail with cracked black pepper and marinate it in the refrigerator for at least 12 hours and up to 2 days.

Prepare a hot grill or get a grill pan very hot. Salt the quail, then grill them, about 2 minutes per side for medium. Serve the quail drizzled with aged balsamic vinegar and garnished with fresh herb sprigs if desired.

chicken with pancetta and sage

SERVES 4

I am not a big fan of skinless chicken breasts and don't use them much, but I make an exception here. I add flavor with sage and create a delicious protective "skin" with pancetta. Set things up a day ahead. Chilling the pancetta-wrapped chicken overnight helps maintain an even shape during cooking and ensures that the pancetta adheres.

Be aware that once formed and chilled, the breasts are very dense, so render and crisp the outer layer of pancetta slowly so the heat has time to penetrate. When it's nicely browned, let the chicken rest and then slice it. You wind up with disks of moist, flavorful chicken encased in the crispest, tastiest skin imaginable.

About ½ pound pancetta, thinly sliced and uncoiled

24 small sage leaves

Kosher salt and freshly ground black pepper

4 medium boneless, skinless chicken breasts (about 7 ounces each)

About 2 tablespoons extra virgin olive oil

You can substitute thinly sliced bacon for the pancetta.

Depending on the size of the pancetta, lay 3 or 4 slices on a clean work surface so that they overlap and form a wide enough sheet to completely enclose a chicken breast. Arrange 3 sage leaves across the sheet of pancetta. Salt and pepper one of the breasts. Fold the tender in (the small loose flap of meat on the underside). Place the breast on the sage leaves and arrange 3 more sage leaves on top. Fold the pancetta around the chicken breast, then wrap the breast in plastic, twisting the ends to form a tight, compact log. Repeat with the remaining chicken breasts, then chill overnight.

About 30 minutes before you wish to eat, remove the chicken from the refrigerator. Heat a skillet large enough to hold the breasts in a roomy single layer over high heat. When the pan is hot, add a skim of oil, about 2 tablespoons. Take the chicken out of the plastic. Place the breasts in the pan so the seam, the loose edge of the folded pancetta, is on the bottom and cooks first.

(recipe continues)

Allow the pan to heat back up. When it begins to sizzle, about 2 minutes, lower the heat to medium. Allow the pancetta to brown, about 2 minutes more, then turn each breast a quarter turn. Gradually brown the meat on all sides (turn each breast at least 4 times), about 20 minutes in all. Remove the pan from the heat. Let the chicken sit in the pan off the stove for 3 minutes, then flip each breast and let it sit for 3 minutes more. Slice into nice thick disks and serve.

roasted cornish hen with lemon and onion

SERVES 4 GENEROUSLY

In this recipe, I pot-roast hens with onions and lemon, which I then puree to make a sauce. The results are super tasty, but you'd never guess that based on the Italian name for this dish: pollo arrosto morbido. The name is a reference to the fact that the hens' skins, though brown, are soft like those of the recently deceased (an interesting comparison but not so appetizing).

4 small Cornish hens (about 1 pound each)

Kosher salt and freshly ground black pepper

2 lemons, 1 quartered, 1 sliced

5 small fresh rosemary sprigs

About ¼ cup extra virgin olive oil

2 medium onions, peeled, halved, and sliced

4 garlic cloves, peeled and crushed

½ cup dry white wine

If you have a big, high-sided, ovenproof skillet, use it. If not, brown the birds, then transfer them to a Dutch oven or roasting pan. Foil works as a cover if you don't have a lid that fits closely.

Season the hens inside and out with salt and pepper. Insert 1 lemon quarter and a rosemary sprig into each hen.

Preheat the oven to 375°F. Heat a skim of oil, about 2 tablespoons, in a large skillet over high heat. Brown the hens (in batches, if necessary), turning to get even color all over, about 10 minutes. Set the hens aside.

Add the onions, remaining rosemary sprig, 2 tablespoons oil, lemon slices, and garlic to the pan. Season with salt and pepper, and mix well. Cook over high heat, stirring occasionally, until the onions begin to soften, about 4 minutes.

The sauce consistency will vary depending on the hens and vegetables. If your sauce seems too loose, it is okay to reduce it in a saucepan over high heat for a few minutes. If it is too thick, add a little Easter Broth (page 8) or water.

Arrange the hens on the onions. Add the wine, cover the pan tightly, and transfer it to the oven. Roast the hens until they are cooked through and their juices run clear, about 30 minutes. Transfer the hens to a platter.

Remove and discard all but two of the lemon slices from the onion mixture, then pass it through a food mill using the medium-holed disk. Add any juices that have accumulated under the hens and adjust the seasoning with salt and pepper. Cut the hens into halves or quarters. Spoon the sauce over them and serve.

pan-roasted duck breast

SERVES 2

Like most poultry, duck breasts cook much more quickly than thighs—so it's best to divide and conquer. I like the breast pan-roasted. Ducks have a substantial layer of fat under the skin; to render it and leave the skin nice and brown, score the skin side and put the breast in a cold pan over moderate heat. Be patient, pouring off excess fat as it accumulates. Once the fat cooks out, the skin will crisp, forming a perfect contrast to the lean, red, juicy meat. I like duck breast cooked medium-rare, then sliced thinly, like steak. The meat is delicious warm but also cold in salads and sandwiches.

1 large magret duck breast (about 13 ounces)
Kosher salt and freshly ground black pepper

Score the skin of the duck, making crosshatch incisions through the fat but stopping short of the flesh. Season the duck on both sides with salt and pepper.

Put the duck in a small cold skillet. Put the pan on the stove and render the fat over medium heat. When the edges begin to color and the breast begins to contract and plump, about 5 minutes, discard the rendered fat. Return the pan to the stove and continue cooking until the skin is crisp (pouring off excess fat as necessary), about 7 minutes more.

Flip the duck over and allow it to finish cooking in the pan but off the heat, 5 minutes for medium-rare. Remove the breast from the pan and allow it to rest in a warm place for 5 minutes. Slice and divide between 2 plates.

spiced magret with honey

Render the fat as described above. When you flip the duck, sprinkle the meat and pan drippings with a mixture of toasted and ground spices. I like a combo of cardamom, star anise, and coriander. You will need only about ½ tablespoon total to flavor the breast. Off the heat, baste the meat with the pan juices. Just before serving, lightly paint the skin with honey, then slice and serve.

Here I've used a meaty magret breast, which is sold individually packaged at butcher and specialty shops, but think about buying a whole duck and braising the legs (see Braised Duck with Niçoise Olives and Rosemary on page 200). It's more economical, and you can make a wonderful stock with the bones or just add them to Easter Broth (page 8).

braising: a forgiving cooking method

Braising is a term generally used to refer to a way of cooking tough cuts of meat by first browning them, then simmering them in broth until tender. Italians use this procedure, but they also use a number of modified braising methods, all useful to know.

Let me map the various ways I braise by focusing first on what I call the "braise and glaze" method. This is the way I most often cook tough cuts like Braised Veal Breast (page 225). The procedure is straightforward: Brown the meat whole or in large pieces. Brown aromatic vegetables, return the meat to the pan, and add liquid—wine, water, broth, or stock—then simmer. When the meat is tender, take the pot off the heat. After it cools, put the meat in a new container and strain the liquid over it. Refrigerate overnight. The meat will firm, the sauce will gel, and the fat will harden on the surface.

The next day, preheat the oven. Skim the fat from the braising liquid and portion the meat (it's easier to cut when it's chilled). Put the meat in a pan and add enough braising liquid to come about halfway up the sides of the meat. Warm the meat in the oven, basting frequently. The finished meat is rich and gorgeous. The braise and glaze method is ideal for restaurants because most of the work is done in advance. But it's also a great way to cook for a party at home.

A more traditional approach to braising tough meat can be seen in the recipe for Short Ribs in Barolo (page 208). Start off as you would for braise and glaze, but rather than chilling, portioning, and glazing the meat, once it is tender, pass the vegetables and braising liquid together through a food mill to create a *passatta* sauce. The vegetables thicken the sauce. The finished dish, which you can serve immediately or save and reheat, is a little rough and nicely robust.

At the other end of the spectrum are what I call "quick braises" and Italians call cooking *in umido*—a great way to cook vegetables or fish. The main thing to remember here is that you have less opportunity to flavor the main ingredient, so you need a richly developed soffritto (page 12). Stewed Romano Beans (page 121) is a perfect example of a quick braise.

Between braise and glaze and quick braise are a number of hybrids. I "stew" (for lack of a better word) tender meat like rabbit or chicken and tougher meat cut into smaller pieces (see Veal and Peppers, page 232). Stovetop stewing has its roots in Italian home cooking, it's not a 2-day process, and there's no straining and less fussing. The recipe for Braised Duck with Niçoise Olives and Rosemary (page 200) is another hybrid—essentially a quick braise and glaze. Because duck legs are pretty lean and tender, so you can take a shortcut, braising and glazing the duck simultaneously in the oven.

Braising is a great way to cook. All these methods are low maintenance and forgiving. All permit the cook considerable room to experiment and adapt. The recipes scattered throughout the book will offer inspiration the next time you're cooking a tough cut like short ribs or veal breast and also some ideas that you can use to cook poultry, fish, and vegetables in interesting ways.

braised duck with niçoise olives and rosemary

SERVES 4

Here the duck is oven-braised, so it braises and glazes simultaneously. The same technique works equally well with all tender meats and poultry (try rabbit, chicken, or even lamb shanks). Delicious straight from the oven, this recipe is, in addition, the starting point for duck ragù (see Pappardelle with Duck Ragù, page 46). What I do at home is braise more than I need and wind up with two very different but equally tasty meals.

8 duck legs

Kosher salt and freshly ground black pepper

About 2 tablespoons extra virgin olive oil

1 medium onion, peeled and minced

1 carrot, peeled and minced

2 celery stalks, minced

1 tablespoon tomato paste

2 fresh rosemary sprigs, leaves picked

1 cup dry red wine

½ cup pitted Niçoise olives

About 4 cups Easter Broth (page 8) or chicken broth

If you have Blond Soffritto Base (page 12), heat 1½ cups, add the tomato paste and rosemary, and proceed as described.

To make sure the braising liquid doesn't become too salty, season the duck before cooking, then hold off adding any more salt until just before serving.

Preheat the oven to 325°F. Season the duck with salt and pepper. Heat a skim of oil, about 2 tablespoons, over medium-high heat in an ovenproof skillet large enough to hold the duck in a snug single layer. Working in batches, brown the duck legs, skin side down, about 7 minutes. Flip them and then brown the other side, about 4 minutes more. Reserve the browned duck legs on a plate.

Discard most of the oil, leaving just enough to coat the bottom of the skillet. Add the onion, carrot, and celery. Fry the vegetables, stirring frequently and adjusting the heat if necessary to prevent burning, until they soften and become a richly caramelized brown, about 12 minutes. Add the tomato paste and rosemary and cook, stirring frequently, until it concentrates and darkens, about 5 minutes. Deglaze the pan with wine, scraping the bottom with a spoon. Return the duck to the pan, skin side down, adding any juices that have accumulated on the plate. Add the olives and enough broth to barely cover.

Bring the broth to a simmer, then transfer the uncovered pan to the oven. Braise the duck in the oven, checking to make sure the liquid is simmering very gently. After 45 minutes, turn the legs over and continue cooking, basting the duck with the braising liquid every 10 minutes until the meat is beginning to shrink from the bone, about 45 minutes more. (At this point, the duck can be cooled in the braising liquid and then separated from the bones and used to make Duck Ragù, page 46.)

Spoon off and discard any fat that floats on the surface of the braising liquid. Adjust the seasoning with salt and pepper and serve in warm shallow bowls.

Braise a day ahead. It's not necessary, but it's a good idea when you can because the fat is easy to remove and the flavors blend and mellow.

rabbit stew with niçoise olives and rosemary

SERVES 4

This is a typically Tuscan dish. It smells so good while it's cooking and tastes even better. Although this dish and the Braised Duck with Niçoise Olives and Rosemary (page 200) sound almost identical, they are in fact quite different. The duck is oven-braised and the finished dish richly browned and glazed. Here the rabbit, stewed on top of the stove, winds up much more brightly flavored. Try these two dishes (or follow each recipe, substituting chicken legs and thighs). You'll not only make delicious meals but will also experience firsthand the range of moist-heat cooking.

2 small rabbits, cut into 10 pieces each (see Notes)
Kosher salt and freshly ground black pepper
About 7 tablespoons extra virgin olive oil
1 cup dry red wine
1 medium onion, peeled and minced
1 carrot, peeled and minced
2 celery stalks, minced
2 tablespoons tomato paste
1 bunch of rosemary sprigs, tied together
About 5½ cups Easter Broth (page 8) or chicken broth
½ cup Niçoise olives, pitted if desired

If you have Blond Soffritto Base (page 12), heat about 1½ cups in place of the minced vegetables. Add the tomato paste and rosemary and continue as described.

Have your butcher cut up the rabbit or do it yourself. If you choose to do it yourself, divide the hind legs into two pieces each, separating the thigh from the leg. Cut the loins in half and the racks in half; leave the front legs whole.

Season the rabbit pieces with salt and pepper. Heat enough oil to coat the bottom of a large skillet, about 3 tablespoons, over medium-high heat. Working in batches, brown the rabbit pieces, about 3 minutes on each side, then set aside in a bowl.

When all of the meat is browned, add the wine and deglaze the pan, scraping up the fond (browned bits) with a wooden spoon. Allow the wine to simmer for a minute or two, then pour it over the browned rabbit and reserve.

Wipe out the skillet. Add the remaining 4 tablespoons oil and heat over medium-high heat. Add the onion, carrot, and celery. Fry the soffritto, stirring frequently and adjusting the heat if necessary to prevent burning, until the vegetables soften and color, about 10 minutes. Add the tomato paste and rosemary. Stir to coat the vegetables and cook until the paste darkens, about 5 minutes.

Return the rabbit and wine to the pan, lower the heat to medium, and stir to mix. Cook the rabbit, stirring occasionally, until its juices release, about 10 minutes.

Add enough broth to come a little less than halfway up the rabbit pieces, about 2 cups. Simmer the rabbit partially covered, turning it in the pan and basting it occasionally, until the pan is almost dry, about 15 minutes. Add more broth, about 1 cup, and continue simmering and basting the rabbit, adding a little broth whenever the pan looks dry (expect to add ½ cup about every 15 minutes). Stew until the rabbit is almost tender, about 1 hour.

Flip the rabbit pieces over and add the olives. Continue adding broth a little at a time and simmer until the rabbit is fully tender, about 15 minutes more (if the meat pulls easily from the leg bone, the rabbit is done). Adjust the seasoning with salt and pepper, reduce the heat to low, and cook for 5 more minutes to allow the seasoning to penetrate. Serve warm in shallow bowls.

You can vary the stew by adding other complementary ingredients along with or instead of the olives. Sliced braised artichokes, roasted pearl or cipollini onions, and pan-roasted mushrooms all work well.

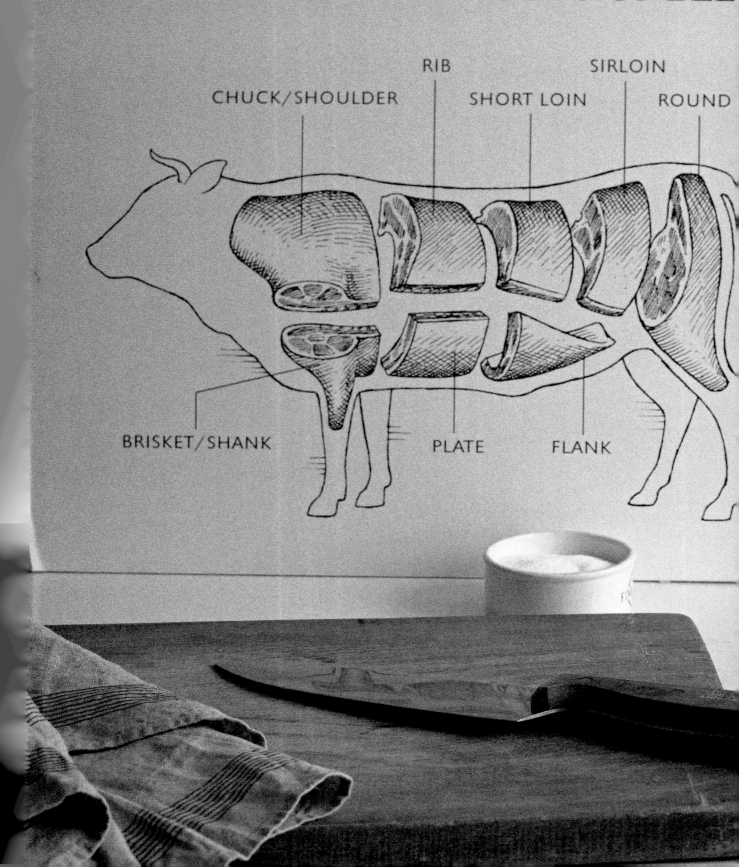

THE EIGHT PRIMAL CUTS OF BEE

CHUCK/SHOULDER

RIB

SHORT LOIN

SIRLOIN

ROUND

BRISKET/SHANK

PLATE

FLANK

meat

cows, pigs, and sheep are, from a cook's standpoint, constructed in very much the same way. The shoulders, necks, and haunches, because they bear weight, are sinuous and tougher than their midsections, where you find the chops, steaks, and loins. Regardless of what kind of meat you're talking about, certain cooking methods work for the midsection cuts, while others work best for the tougher parts of the animal.

The midsection cuts are naturally tender and the biggest worry is drying the meat out, so a relatively quick, dry-heat cooking method like sautéing, grilling, or roasting works beautifully. Tougher (usually cheaper) cuts need to be softened but are less likely to dry out, because the connective tissue that makes them hard to chew will melt, lubricating the meat during cooking. This makes thorough, slow methods better, and penetrating moist-heat methods like braising best of all.

You can substitute a cut of meat from one animal in a recipe for the corresponding cut from another—you can cook a veal chop the same way you cook a lamb chop, and ribs of pork can be substituted for ribs of beef. Yes, there are differences in flavor, fat content, and size, but all of these are easily addressed by changing an ingredient here or there and altering the cooking time. If you really consider and apply what I'm saying, you will have multiplied your culinary repertoire instantly.

Another thing that causes confusion is how the USDA grades meat. Three grades of meat are sold in the United States: prime, choice, and select, the lowest of the three. The Agriculture Department grades meat based on a number of factors; the most important as far as cooks are concerned is the amount of marbling—how evenly the fat is distributed through the meat. If you are buying a tender cut, like a rib eye or sirloin, and plan to cook it medium-rare, you should buy prime meat, because the well-distributed fat will flavor the meat and keep it from drying out. The extra money you spend will be worth it. It's not nearly so important to buy the best if you are going to braise a tough cut like breast of veal. At the supermarket, you are likely to find select and choice meats. If you want prime meat, you will have to go to the butcher or a specialty store.

short ribs in barolo

SERVES 4

Marinating the meat overnight allows the flavor to penetrate and deepen.

Beef in Barolo is a classic preparation from Piedmont. It's characteristic of Italian farmhouse cooking both in the simplicity of the approach and the depth of flavor it produces. The rich and flavorful sauce is the heart of the dish. It's a passato—sauce made by using the aromatic vegetables braised with the meat as a thickener by passing them with the braising liquid through a food mill (in Italian, passare means to pass through). It's a great rustic technique I also use in the recipe for Roasted Cornish Hen with Lemon and Onion (page 196). I should mention that a good Barolo, or in fact any Barolo at all, is not essential here. I grab a reasonably priced dry red for the pot and save the Barolo to drink when I'm done.

I've seen short ribs cut a million different ways— every butcher seems to do it differently. It really doesn't matter, but remember to adjust the cooking time up or down based on the size and shape of the pieces of meat you're using. In fact, you can use any stew beef—shoulder, shank, oxtail—although I like short ribs best because the high fat content makes them particularly moist and succulent.

4 whole short ribs on the bone (about 4 pounds)

1½ cups dry red wine

3 tablespoons extra virgin olive oil

Kosher salt and freshly ground black pepper

2 large onions, peeled and diced

4 medium carrots, peeled and diced

6 celery stalks, diced

3 large garlic cloves, peeled and crushed

2 fresh rosemary sprigs

4 fresh thyme sprigs

About 1 cup Easter Broth (page 8), chicken broth, or water

Combine the ribs and wine in a bowl, cover with plastic wrap, and marinate in the refrigerator overnight. Drain the ribs and reserve the marinade.

Preheat the oven to 350°F. Heat the oil in a large high-sided ovenproof skillet or Dutch oven over medium-high heat. Working in batches, season the ribs with salt and pepper and brown them on all sides, about 10 minutes. Transfer the browned ribs to a plate.

Add the onions, carrots, celery, and garlic to the pot and reduce the heat to medium-low. Cook, stirring frequently, until the vegetables soften and brown nicely, about 15 minutes. Season the vegetables conservatively with salt and pepper and return the meat to the pot. Add the rosemary and thyme.

Take the time to brown the meat thoroughly on all sides—this helps deep flavor to develop. And choose a pot that holds everything in a snug single layer. For more about braising, see page 198.

Raise the heat to high and add the wine. Boil it, scraping up the fond (browned bits) on the bottom of the pot until the wine all but completely evaporates, about 30 seconds. Add enough broth or water to surround but not quite cover the meat. Bring the liquid to a simmer, then cover the pot and transfer it to the oven.

Braise the meat for 1½ hours. Remove the lid and continue cooking until the ribs are very tender, about 30 minutes more (the cooking time will vary depending on how the ribs were cut; just be patient and let them go until they're fork-tender).

Using a slotted spoon, carefully transfer the ribs to a plate (the meat has a tendency to fall off the bone—it's okay if it does, but you'll have a more dramatic presentation if it doesn't). Bring the braising liquid with the vegetables to a simmer on top of the stove. Skim off the layer of fat on the surface, leaving a few tablespoons for flavor.

I use a food mill to make the sauce because it separates the fiber from the flesh of the vegetables as you puree. Pureeing in a blender or food processor and then passing the sauce through a fine sieve will work, but the flavor and texture will be different.

Place a food mill over a clean saucepan. Pass the sauce through the mill. Taste the sauce and adjust the seasoning and texture (reduce it if it is too thin and add a little water if it is too thick). Warm the meat in the sauce on top of the stove, then serve.

braised beef involtini

SERVES 6

Involtini are stuffed rolls of tender meat. You can use almost any kind: poultry, pork, veal, or beef, and the stuffing possibilities are nearly endless. In this case, I start with beef top round, a very lean cut, pounding it thin and then wrapping it around sausage. The flavorful filling keeps the beef moist during the cooking—a braise in broth with cabbage. When you're done, you wind up with a hearty dish that for me perfectly combines the tastes and textures of the lean dry beef, rich sausage, and meltingly tender cabbage.

2 pounds beef top round (have your butcher cut
    and pound 18 slices)

¾ pound sausage, casing removed

2½ tablespoons finely chopped fresh sage

1 tablespoon minced garlic

About 5 tablespoons extra virgin olive oil

Kosher salt and freshly ground black pepper

¾ cup dry white wine

2 small onions, peeled and minced

1 celery stalk, minced

1 small carrot, peeled and minced

1 fresh sage sprig

1 fresh rosemary sprig

2½ tablespoons tomato paste

1 medium head of savoy cabbage, quartered, cored,
    ribs removed, and leaves cut into large pieces

About 3 cups Easter Broth (page 8) or chicken broth

Put 3 pounded slices of beef on a clean work surface. Spread a heaping teaspoon of sausage on each piece of meat. Sprinkle a little sage and garlic over each, then roll tightly; secure with a toothpick. Repeat filling and rolling all the involtini.

Coat the bottom of a large high-sided skillet with oil, about 3 tablespoons, and heat over medium-high heat. Season the rolls with salt and pepper.

(recipe continues)

Working in batches if necessary, brown them on all sides, about 5 minutes. Add the wine to the skillet and deglaze, scraping the fond (the browned bits) from the bottom of the pan. Transfer the meat and any pan juices remaining to a plate.

Wipe out the pan and add 2 tablespoons of oil. Heat over medium. Add the onions, celery, carrot, sage sprig, and rosemary. Cook, stirring occasionally, over medium heat until the vegetables are golden, about 20 minutes. Add the tomato paste and cook, stirring, until it concentrates, about 2 minutes.

Add the cabbage to the skillet. Stir to mix the cabbage with the vegetables. Return the browned beef rolls to the pan and let everything cook together until the cabbage wilts and the meat heats through, about 10 minutes.

Add enough broth to come about two-thirds of the way up the meat, about 1½ cups, and bring to a simmer. Reduce the heat to medium-low, season with salt and pepper, and simmer gently, adding more broth whenever the pan looks dry. Cook until the cabbage is very tender, about 40 minutes. Spoon the involtini, cabbage, and broth into shallow bowls and serve.

Feel free to make this dish several hours ahead. Reheat over medium-low heat just before serving.

stove-top rib eye

SERVES 2

Many people feel that the only way to cook a good steak is to sear it over hot coals or cook it in a supercharged steak house oven. I'd like to suggest a really easy, indoor alternative that I think is even better. My way, you get a perfect medium-rare throughout, unlike a seared steak, where the ends wind up somewhere between medium and well done. What you do is cook the steak in a skillet—an old black cast iron if you have it—on top of the stove. You have to manage the heat—don't blast it—so you hear a nice even sizzle as the meat cooks. Help things along by basting the meat with the pan juices, garlic, and thyme toward the end. It takes a little longer, but the steak winds up tender, juicy, and very flavorful.

About 2 tablespoons extra virgin olive oil

1 rib-eye steak, 1" thick (about 1 pound)

Kosher salt and freshly ground black pepper

2 unpeeled garlic cloves

2 fresh thyme sprigs

2 tablespoons unsalted butter

Get a skillet very hot over high heat and add a skim of oil, about 2 tablespoons. Season the meat on both sides with salt and pepper and add it to the skillet. Lower the heat to medium. Cook the steak, adjusting the heat if necessary to maintain a gentle sizzle, until you begin to see color creep halfway up the side of the meat and the edges begin to brown, about 5 minutes.

Flip the steak over. Crush the garlic cloves with a knife and add them and the thyme to the skillet. Continue cooking the meat until it begins to feel a little firmer when poked, about 3 minutes. Add the butter and finish cooking the meat, tilting the pan toward you and basting it with the melting butter and pan juices, until it is done to your liking, about 2 minutes more for medium-rare. Transfer the steak to a plate, cover it loosely with foil, and allow it to rest for 5 minutes in a warm place. Slice and serve.

Always rest a steak after you cook it. This allows the juices, drawn toward the surface during cooking, to redistribute back through the meat, making the steak much tastier and juicier.

scaloppine remembered

You don't see veal scaloppine on menus as much as you used to. There was a time that every Italian restaurant offered a long list: scaloppine al marsala, scaloppine piccata, scaloppine al limone, and so on, along with a remarkably similar list of dishes featuring chicken in place of the veal. My first restaurant job was at The Ship Lantern Inn in Milton, New York. It was a typical old-school place advertising "continental cuisine." We had a menu full of scaloppine, and I have to say, it was good. We cooks got together what we needed for all the classic sauces—wine, lemon juice, shallots, garlic, mushrooms, peas, peppers, herbs—then quickly sautéed pounded veal and made the sauce right in the pan. The whole thing took under 5 minutes, then we'd wipe out the skillets and start again.

I already knew and loved these dishes; I'd grown up eating them all. They were simple, quick to make, almost infinitely variable, and delicious.

A proper scallop is cut from the top round of veal, against the grain, a little over $\frac{1}{8}$ inch thick. Then it's pounded so it's about half as thick. The unfortunate truth is a lot of butchers don't get it right, and those who do charge for it, but because the veal is pounded and sauced, 4 ounces is a generous serving, which makes its relatively high cost per pound easier to live with.

To make the pounded cutlets more manageable, cut each portion into pieces about the size of your fist—there'll be two or three per serving. Then get everything ready for the sauce. Chop the shallots, garlic, and herbs and make sure the wine, butter, and whatever else you're going to need are at hand—this is essential because the cooking goes really fast.

When you've got everything ready, heat your pan and flour the cutlets. This helps them brown and adds a little body to the sauce. Cook them in batches over high heat. As soon as the last piece of veal is done, start the sauce. Again, the sauce goes fast. Sauté your shallots; add in capers, olives, herbs, or whatever flavorings you're using and then deglaze with wine. If your deglazing liquid has evaporated and the pan looks dry, add a couple of tablespoons of broth or water before you start adding butter. Take the pan off the heat, and swirl in cold butter a tablespoon at a time. Pour the sauce over the meat and serve.

Think of the recipes that follow as templates for making exactly what you want. Change the deglazing liquid, swirl in a little mustard, or add peas, roasted peppers, or braised artichokes at the end. You can also substitute cheaper alternatives like pounded chicken breast or pork loin if you like.

veal marsala

SERVES 4

Marsala is a fortified Italian wine. You will find sweet and dry varieties at your wine shop; for this recipe, you want a dry Marsala. I like to add mushrooms to my sauce. I pan-roast them ahead and have them ready to go. Fresh porcini are amazing but expensive; button mushrooms work just fine. I usually wind up somewhere in the middle, with an assortment of wild and cultivated mushrooms. If you do use more than one kind, cook each variety separately (for more about cleaning and pan-roasting mushrooms, see page 145).

1 pound mushrooms

About 7 tablespoons unsalted butter

About 4 tablespoons extra virgin olive oil

Kosher salt and freshly ground black pepper

1 pound veal cutlets, pounded thin and cut into 8 pieces
    (for more about veal scaloppine, see page 214)

2 teaspoons finely chopped fresh rosemary

1 cup all-purpose flour

½ cup dry Marsala wine

2 tablespoons Easter Broth (page 8) or chicken broth

Trim the mushrooms and cut them into slices, all about the same size. Heat 2 tablespoons butter and 1 tablespoon oil in a large skillet over high heat. Add about half of the mushrooms (the number and size of each batch will depend on the kind of mushrooms you are cooking). Season with salt and pepper and cook the mushrooms until they begin to brown, about 5 minutes. Flip the mushrooms and cook until they're tender, about 3 minutes more. Transfer the mushrooms to a bowl, wipe out the skillet, and repeat, adding more butter and oil for each batch. Reserve the cooked mushrooms.

Sprinkle the veal with 1½ teaspoons rosemary and season with salt and pepper. Press the rosemary into the meat, then lightly flour each cutlet; shake off the excess flour.

Heat a large skillet over high heat. Add 1 tablespoon butter and 1 tablespoon oil. When the butter melts and foams, add about half of the veal. Cook until the veal is golden, about 1 minute. Flip the meat and cook the other side, about 30 seconds more; transfer to a serving plate. Wipe out the pan. Add more butter and oil to the pan and cook the rest of the meat. Reserve the meat in a warm place covered loosely with foil.

When all the veal is cooked, add the mushrooms and the remaining ½ tea-spoon rosemary to the hot pan. Let the pan heat back up, about 3 minutes, then deglaze with Marsala, scraping up any fond (browned bits) sticking to the pan. Cook until the wine has reduced and evaporated and then add the broth (you'll need to use a little more if your pan is very large or very hot). Allow the broth to boil down until it thickens, about 30 seconds, then take the pan off the heat and swirl in the remaining 1 tablespoon butter. Adjust the seasoning with salt and pepper. Pour the sauce over the meat and serve.

Be careful when you add the Marsala to the pan; if it is very hot, the Marsala will flame.

veal piccata

SERVES 4

This is a classic scaloppine recipe with a simple bright sauce of shallots, lemon juice, white wine, capers, and parsley. Adding a little broth at the end helps the sauce emulsify.

1 pound veal cutlets, pounded thin and cut into 8 pieces

Kosher salt and freshly ground black pepper

1 cup all-purpose flour

6 tablespoons (¾ stick) unsalted butter

2 tablespoons extra virgin olive oil

3 tablespoons minced or thinly sliced shallots

½ cup dry white wine

2 tablespoons Easter Broth (page 8) or chicken broth

Juice of 1 lemon

2½ tablespoons drained capers

2 tablespoons finely chopped fresh flat-leaf parsley

Season the meat with salt and pepper. Lightly flour each cutlet.

Heat a large skillet over high heat. Add 2 tablespoons butter and 1 tablespoon oil. When the butter melts and foams, add about half of the veal—you want to fill but not crowd the pan. Cook until the veal is golden, about 1 minute. Flip the meat and cook the other side for 30 seconds more. Transfer the veal to a serving plate. Wipe out the pan. Add more butter and oil and cook the rest of the meat, taking care to adjust the heat as necessary as you go. Reserve loosely covered with foil.

Be careful when you add the wine to the pan; if it is very hot, the wine may flame.

Add the shallots to the same skillet. Cook over low heat until they soften, stirring and swirling the pan so they don't burn, about 1 minute. Add the wine and deglaze the pan over high heat, scraping the fond (browned bits) from the pan. When the pan is almost dry, add the broth and then the lemon juice, capers, and parsley. When the sauce has reduced and thickened, about 30 seconds, remove the pan from the heat and swirl in the remaining 2 tablespoons butter, 1 tablespoon at a time. Adjust the seasoning with salt and pepper. Pour the sauce over the meat and serve.

veal cutlet milanese

SERVES 4

Make sure you pat off any excess flour before you dip the cutlets in egg. Press the bread crumbs onto the meat with your hands. Serve simply with a squeeze of lemon or try topping the crisp veal with an arugula salad, another classic option.

> 1 pound veal cutlets, pounded thin and cut into 8 pieces
> (for more about veal scaloppine, see page 214)
>
> Kosher salt and freshly ground black pepper
>
> 1 tablespoon finely chopped fresh sage
>
> 1½ cups all-purpose flour
>
> 3 eggs
>
> 1½ cups unseasoned bread crumbs
>
> About 2 tablespoons unsalted butter
>
> About 2 tablespoons extra virgin olive oil
>
> 1 lemon, cut into quarters

Season the meat with salt and pepper. Press the sage into the meat.

Set up a breading station. Put the flour on a plate and beat the eggs in a wide shallow bowl; season both with salt and pepper. Put the bread crumbs on a plate and season them with salt and pepper.

Dip the cutlets into the flour, shake off the excess, and use a fork to dip them into the egg; follow with the bread crumbs. Pat the bread crumbs into the meat with your hands. Put the breaded veal on a large plate. For the best results, chill the cutlets for at least 20 minutes.

Heat 1 tablespoon butter and 1 tablespoon oil in a large skillet over medium-high heat. When the butter is melted and foaming, add half of the cutlets to the pan in a single layer. Cook until the cutlets are golden, about 2 minutes. Flip and cook until the second side is also golden, about 2 minutes more. Transfer the fried cutlets to a plate lined with paper towels to drain. Season them with salt. Wipe out the pan and repeat with the remaining cutlets, butter, and oil. Serve immediately garnished with fresh lemon.

It is best to keep your fingers dry during the breading process, so use a fork to dip the cutlets into the egg.

Chilling the breaded cutlets in the refrigerator for 20 minutes or so before you cook them helps ensure that the crust adheres.

veal cutlet lucchese

SERVES 4

The term scaloppine is used to refer to veal cutlet sautéed and served with a pan sauce. It is also sometimes used to simply refer to the cutlet that here I bread then fry.

This approach to breading and frying veal cutlets is typical of the Tuscan town of Lucca. The cutlets (at left in the photo opposite) are first breaded and then dipped in egg, and wind up soft, tender, and wonderfully rich. It's what I grew up on. Veal Cutlet Milanese, the recipe that precedes this one and is at right in the photo opposite, offers the approach preferred in Lombardy, in which the cutlets are floured, dipped in egg, and then finished with a coating of bread crumbs, resulting in a crispier cutlet. Both are good, and both are worth knowing.

1 pound veal cutlets, pounded thin and cut into 8 pieces

Kosher salt and freshly ground black pepper

1 tablespoon finely chopped fresh sage

1½ cups unseasoned bread crumbs

3 eggs

2 tablespoons unsalted butter

2 tablespoons extra virgin olive oil

1 lemon, cut into quarters

Season the meat with salt and pepper. Press sage into each piece.

Set up a breading station. Put the bread crumbs on a plate and season them with salt and pepper. Beat the eggs in a wide shallow bowl and season them with salt and pepper.

Dip the cutlets into the bread crumbs, pressing the crumbs into the meat firmly with your hands. Allow the excess crumbs to fall away, then dip the cutlets into the eggs, allowing the extra to drip back into the bowl.

Heat 1 tablespoon butter and 1 tablespoon oil in a large skillet over medium-high heat. When the butter is melted and foaming, add a single layer of veal. Cook until the cutlets are brown, about 2 minutes. Flip and cook until the second side is also brown, about 2 minutes more. Transfer the fried cutlets to a plate lined with paper towels to drain. Wipe out the pan and repeat with the remaining cutlets, butter, and oil. Serve immediately garnished with fresh lemon.

veal and ricotta meatballs
in tomato sauce

SERVES 4

There's no getting around the fact that this recipe is a pain in the neck. You have to start a day ahead, keep your meat chilled, and really can't take shortcuts. No doubt you're thinking that a recipe for something as homey as meatballs shouldn't be picky and complicated. In theory I agree, but I have to tell you, these meatballs are worth it.

The veal must be triple ground for extra smoothness—a butcher can do this or you can do it at home (three times through the meat grinder, no need to change the die), and the ricotta must be thoroughly drained overnight.

1 pound fresh ricotta cheese

1 pound ground veal (have the butcher triple grind the veal or pass it through a meat grinder), chilled

2 eggs

1 cup freshly grated Parmigiano-Reggiano plus additional for serving

1 tablespoon of kosher salt plus additional for seasoning the sauce

Freshly ground black pepper

Pinch of freshly grated nutmeg

About 1 cup all-purpose flour

Rich Tomato Sauce (page 20)

Vegetable oil for frying

Spoon the ricotta onto a large piece of cheesecloth; gather the sides together around the cheese and tie closed. Place the wrapped cheese in a sieve set over a bowl. Weight the cheese and refrigerate overnight to drain.

Combine the ricotta, veal, eggs, and Parmigiano in a large bowl. Season the mixture with 1 tablespoon salt, a generous amount of pepper, and nutmeg. Mix vigorously (it's best to use your hands) until completely smooth, pale, and homogenized, about 4 minutes.

Test the seasoning by poaching a pinch of the mixture in simmering water (this is a truer test of the level of seasoning than frying). It should taste assertively salty (braising the meatballs in tomato sauce tames the seasoning). If the sample is too bland, add a little more salt and mix again. Chill the mixture thoroughly before shaping into meatballs.

(recipe continues)

The meatball mixture contains no bread, so it's fragile, and if the meat is too coarse or the cheese too wet, the meatballs will break up during cooking. You have to chill the mixture twice: before shaping and then again before frying. At Hearth, we freeze the meatballs to make them easier to handle in the skillet.

The meatballs can be frozen in the sauce, then reheated gently.

Dust a baking sheet and your hands with flour. Keep the remaining flour nearby in a bowl. Gently form the meat into balls about 2½" in diameter, flouring your hands again between meatballs (alternatively, use a floured ice cream scoop to form the meatballs). Arrange the meatballs on the floured baking sheet. There is enough mixture to make 9 meatballs, 2 per person (plus an extra for the cook). Cover the meatballs with plastic wrap and chill or freeze.

Warm the tomato sauce in a large Dutch oven or high-sided skillet over medium-low heat. Season it conservatively with salt and pepper.

Heat about ½" oil in a large skillet over medium-high heat. When the oil is hot, begin carefully frying the meatballs in batches, moving them as little as possible. Cook the meatballs until the bottoms are nicely browned, about 2 minutes, then gently turn them. Continue frying until the meatballs are browned all over, about 10 minutes more. Using a slotted spoon, carefully transfer the meatballs to the pot of tomato sauce.

Finish cooking the meatballs in the tomato sauce, simmering gently over medium-low heat for at least 30 minutes (they can remain in the sauce for hours without ill effect). Taste the sauce and adjust the seasoning with salt and pepper. Serve the meatballs alone or over pasta with additional Parmigiano.

braised veal breast

SERVES 6

There are two things that make all the difference in this recipe: the right liquid and the right pan. You want a broth or stock with a certain amount of gelatin. If you have Easter Broth (page 8) or veal stock, that's great. If not, add ½ cup demiglace (reduced veal stock) to homemade or commercial chicken broth. The demiglace will provide the viscosity necessary to glaze the veal properly at the end of cooking.

As far as the pan goes, you want one just big enough to hold the meat and aromatic vegetables snugly so the broth surrounds but doesn't swamp the meat. This is true whenever you braise, but it's particularly important here. Using a pan that's too big will force you to use too much broth, which will in turn reduce the concentration of flavor and leave you with a weak-tasting, thin sauce. As long as the meat and vegetables fit with room to add broth to cover, the pan is fine.

(recipe continues)

There are several
advantages to making
the veal a day in
advance. 1) Breaking
the cooking into two
parts makes for short
easy work just before
serving. 2) The veal can
be sliced neatly only
when chilled. 3) It is
easier to defat the
chilled braising liquid—
just spoon the fat off
before you reduce the
liquid. In a pinch, you
can forgo these advan-
tages and start and
finish the veal in the
same day. But in that
case, I would advise
you to skip slicing it
and serve it whole—
a dramatic if slightly
more rustic way to go.

½ boneless veal breast (about 2½ pounds)

2 garlic cloves, peeled and minced, plus 1 head cut in half crosswise

2 tablespoons finely chopped fresh rosemary plus 3 sprigs tied together

About 7 tablespoons extra virgin olive oil

Kosher salt and freshly ground black pepper

1 large carrot, peeled and chopped

1 onion, peeled and chopped

2 celery stalks, chopped

1 cup dry white wine

About 2 quarts Easter Broth (page 8) or chicken broth

2 garlic cloves

2 rosemary sprigs

Preheat the oven to 375°F. Lay the meat flat on a clean work surface. Mix the minced garlic, chopped rosemary, and 2 tablespoons oil in a small bowl. Spread evenly over the meat, then season liberally with salt and pepper. Roll the meat into a tight, thick roll, securing it every few inches with butcher's string. Season the outside of the meat with salt and pepper.

Heat a deep pan just big enough to hold the meat over medium-high heat and add enough oil to generously coat the bottom, about 5 tablespoons. Add the veal and brown it on all sides, about 10 minutes. Remove the veal from the pan and reserve.

Add the carrot, onion, celery, and garlic head. Cook, stirring occasionally, until the vegetables brown and soften, about 5 minutes. Return the meat to the pan.

Add the rosemary sprigs and wine. Let the wine boil and reduce until the pan is almost dry, then add enough broth to surround and just barely cover the meat. Bring to a boil on top of the stove, turn the veal over, and put the pan in the oven.

Braise the veal, turning it every 20 to 30 minutes, until it is tender and a knife can be easily inserted and removed (always check the thickest part closest to the center), about 2 hours.

Remove the pan from the oven and allow the veal to cool in the braising liquid. Take the meat out of the pan and put it into another container. Strain the braising liquid over the meat (discard the vegetables). Cover and refrigerate the veal in the braising liquid overnight.

To glaze the veal, preheat the oven to 375°F. Remove the meat from the pan and cut it into slices about ½" thick. Skim the fat from the braising liquid. Put the liquid into a saucepan and bring it to a boil over high heat. Skim frequently and reduce until the liquid is slightly viscous (the amount of time this takes will depend on your broth).

Arrange the veal slices in a roasting pan big enough to hold them in a snug single layer. Pour enough of the reduced braising sauce around the veal so it comes about two-thirds of the way up the meat. Crush the garlic with the flat of a knife and add it along with the rosemary. Baste the veal with sauce and place it in the oven. Glaze the veal, basting it with the sauce every 5 minutes, until it is browned and heated through, about 40 minutes. Serve.

vitello tonnato

SERVES 6 TO 8

Leftover Vitello Tonnato makes a great sandwich, and the tuna puree on its own is good as a bruschetta topping.

I'm always surprised to realize how few people are familiar with this venerable Italian dish. And maybe a little less surprised when I describe it to guests at the restaurant—thinly sliced poached veal marinated in a puree of tuna, capers, and anchovies served sort of like carpaccio—and their faces make clear the description doesn't entice them. But the truth is it's delicious, rich, not at all heavy, a perfect first course or light supper.

FOR THE VEAL:

2 pounds top round veal roast, wrapped in cheesecloth and tied to hold its shape

1 small onion, peeled and halved

4 fresh flat-leaf parsley sprigs

1 bay leaf

Kosher salt

10 black peppercorns

I recommend tuna imported from Italy— it's packed in good olive oil and just has better flavor.

FOR THE SAUCE:

1 (6-ounce) can tuna, preferably Italian, drained

4 anchovy fillets, minced

3 tablespoons drained capers plus additional for serving

Juice of 1 lemon

Kosher salt and freshly ground black pepper

Maionese (page 256)

¼ cup celery leaves

1 medium celery stalk, thinly sliced

You must make the Maionese for this dish; commercial mayonnaise is no substitute.

TO MAKE THE VEAL: Put the veal and onion in a pot that holds them snugly. Add the parsley and bay leaf and enough water to cover by about 1". Season the water with 2 tablespoons salt and plenty of pepper. Partially cover the pot and, over medium-low heat, bring the liquid to just below a simmer (the water should steam but not bubble). Adjust the heat so the water stays just below a simmer and poach the meat until it is cooked through, about 1 hour. Remove the pot from the heat and allow the veal to cool in the braising liquid. Chill the meat with the braising liquid overnight.

TO MAKE THE SAUCE: Combine the tuna, anchovies, and capers in a food processor and puree. Season the puree with lemon juice and lots of pepper. Transfer the tuna puree to a bowl and fold in the maionese, half at a time. Season with salt.

Slice the chilled veal about ⅛" thick. Spoon a little of the sauce onto a serving platter, arrange a layer of veal slices on the platter, then dress them with a little more sauce. Repeat layering veal and sauce, ending with sauce (reserve about ⅓ cup of sauce in the refrigerator for serving). Wrap the platter with plastic and marinate in the refrigerator for up to a week. Serve dressed with the reserved sauce and garnished with celery leaves, sliced celery, and additional capers if desired.

The key to success is allowing the meat to marinate in the flavorful sauce for several hours or, better yet, overnight. The lean veal absorbs the sauce and the whole becomes much more than the predictable combination of the parts.

Other possible garnishes include caper berries, green olives, chopped parsley, cherry tomatoes, lemon zest, and braised artichokes.

osso bucco

SERVES 6

A veal shank is wide at the top and narrows toward the bottom, so if you want all your servings to be the same size, ask the butcher for center cut. At home, I don't bother. I think it's nice to have some variation so people with large appetites are satisfied and less-hearty eaters aren't overwhelmed. Because braising is forgiving, it's fine to cook the small pieces for the same amount of time you cook the larger. I do think it's important that the shanks be cut about 2" thick and that it's necessary to tie some kitchen twine around the circumference of each portion. This holds the shape of the meat and keeps it on the bone, which makes things look nicer at the end.

FOR THE VEAL:

6 (2"-thick) pieces veal shank (about 6½ pounds)

Kosher salt and freshly ground black pepper

About 2 cups all-purpose flour

⅓ cup extra virgin olive oil

1 cup dry white wine

About 3 cups Easter Broth (page 8), chicken broth, or water

FOR THE SOFFRITTO:

About ¼ cup extra virgin olive oil

1½ cups minced red onions

¾ cup minced celery

¾ cup minced carrot

2 garlic cloves, peeled and thinly sliced

6 canned tomatoes

1 small bunch fresh rosemary, tied in a bundle

Strips of peel from 1 lemon, white pith removed

FOR THE GREMOLATA:

Grated zest of 2 lemons

1 cup fresh flat-leaf parsley leaves

1 garlic clove, peeled and chopped (optional)

If you have Blond Soffritto Base (page 12), heat about 1½ cups. Fry it, adding the garlic and tomatoes, and proceed as described.

TO MAKE THE VEAL: Season the veal with salt and pepper, then dredge each piece in flour, shaking off the excess. Heat the oil in a large high-sided ovenproof skillet or Dutch oven over medium-high heat. Working in batches, brown the meat on all sides, about 10 minutes. Return all the meat to the pan.

Raise the heat and pour the wine over the browned meat. Deglaze the pan, scraping up the fond (browned bits) from the bottom of the pan. Allow the wine to boil for a minute or two, then transfer the meat and wine to a bowl.

TO MAKE THE SOFFRITTO: Return the pan to the stove and heat the oil over medium-high heat. Add the onions, celery, and carrot and fry, stirring frequently, for 10 minutes. Reduce the heat to medium and add the garlic. Continue to fry, stirring frequently, until the soffritto begins to color, about 5 minutes. Crush the tomatoes into the pan, allowing the juices to fall into the skillet. Cook, stirring occasionally, until the tomatoes are evenly distributed and incorporated, about 10 minutes more. Add the rosemary and lemon peel.

Preheat the oven to 350°F.

Return the meat and wine to the pan. Add enough broth to surround but not submerge the meat (the top of each piece should protrude a little). Bring the broth to a simmer, then transfer the pan to the oven.

Braise the veal uncovered for about 30 minutes, baste the meat, then braise for 30 minutes more. Turn the veal shanks over and continue braising, basting every 15 minutes or so, until the meat is fork-tender and nicely glazed, about 1 hour more. The osso bucco can be served immediately or refrigerated and reheated.

Shortly before serving, finely chop the lemon zest with the parsley and garlic if using. Serve the osso bucco in warm bowls topped with the gremolata.

monkfish osso bucco

Substitute six 2"-thick medallions of monkfish on the bone (about 4½ pounds) for the veal and proceed as above. The fish will take less time to brown, about 7 minutes. Add only enough broth to come two-thirds up the fish, about 2½ cups. Braise the fish, basting every 10 minutes, until it is tender, about 30 minutes.

Dredging the meat in flour helps it to brown nicely and helps to bind the sauce. Take your time browning the meat—this will help the flavor develop. And take care not to burn the fond on the bottom of the pan.

veal and peppers

SERVES 4 TO 6

Veal and peppers is a great dish to add to your repertoire. This, my mother's version, is a deeply flavored and satisfying dish that is ideal for summer and early fall evenings, when the peppers are perfect. But it's also good in February made with hothouse peppers. Served over polenta, there's pretty much nothing better.

Cubed veal breast is my first choice for this recipe; it has some fat. Shoulder or leg meat also works. Cubed beef, pork, chicken, or lamb can be cooked this way; just be sure to use a stew-worthy cut.

About 5½ tablespoons extra virgin olive oil

3 garlic cloves, peeled and crushed

5 fresh sage leaves plus 1 tablespoon finely chopped sage

1½ pounds boneless veal stew meat

Kosher salt and freshly ground black pepper

¾ cup dry white wine

1 tablespoon tomato paste

About ¾ cup Easter Broth (page 8), chicken broth, or water

2 cups diced red or yellow peppers

2 cups diced onions

1 tablespoon finely chopped fresh rosemary

Combine 3½ tablespoons oil, the garlic, and 5 sage leaves in a large skillet. Heat over high heat. When the garlic and sage begin to brown, about 5 minutes, remove them from the pan and reserve.

While the oil heats, dry the meat on paper towels. Season the meat with salt and pepper and add about half of it to the pan. Cook, turning the meat, until it is browned on all sides, about 7 minutes. Transfer the meat to a bowl with a slotted spoon and brown the second batch.

Return the browned veal and reserved sage and garlic to the skillet. Add the wine and deglaze the pan, scraping up the fond (browned bits) as the wine simmers and reduces.

When the pan is almost dry, add the tomato paste. Stir to coat the meat with the tomato. Cook for a couple of minutes, then add ½ cup broth. Reduce the heat, partially cover the pan, and simmer gently until the meat is almost tender, about 1 hour, adding more broth from time to time to prevent the pan from getting too dry.

Meanwhile, heat a skim of oil, about 2 tablespoons, over high heat in another skillet. Add the peppers and onions, season with salt and pepper, and cook, stirring frequently, until the vegetables begin to soften and caramelize, about 7 minutes. Remove the peppers and onions from the heat.

When the meat is almost (but not quite) tender, add the peppers and onions and the chopped sage and rosemary to the veal. Add enough broth so the pan isn't dry and simmer, partially covered, until the meat is tender and the sauce reduced and glossy, about 30 minutes more. Adjust the seasoning with salt and pepper and serve.

It takes a little over an hour and a half start to finish to make this, but most of that time you don't have to be involved. My mother would cook it after work, but you could just as easily make it a day ahead. This dish also freezes well.

more about stewing

Veal and Peppers is a good example of what I call stewing. It's a Tuscan approach, and the results are nothing like the beef stew the term may conjure up. The method is a variation on braising (see "Braising: A Forgiving Cooking Method" on page 198) and is best suited to more tender meat or tougher meat that's been cut small. Stewing begins by browning meat in fat. Add soffritto, often some tomato, then a small amount of broth, just enough to keep things moist and start a sauce; not so much that the flavors get diluted during the relatively short cooking time. Simmer and baste occasionally. When the pan looks dry, add some more liquid, cooking the stew like you would a risotto. The soffritto becomes a part of the sauce. The stew never swims, the braising liquid concentrates and fortifies, and the end result is deeply satisfying. I use the same method in Rabbit Stew with Niçoise Olives and Rosemary (page 202), but because the meat is quite tender and cooks quite quickly, I am even more careful to add the broth a little at a time.

lamb fricassee

SERVES 4

For as long as I can remember, I've been trying to figure out a way to put this dish on my menu—it's so good. The problem is, the finished dish doesn't look beautiful, an issue in a restaurant but not so much at home. Tender chunks of lamb (I use leg meat) are sautéed with onions, garlic, and herbs, then the fricassee is finished with a simple sauce of lemon and egg. The finished dish looks like a stew but tastes like well-roasted meat with a rich, lemony sauce.

2 tablespoons extra virgin olive oil

2 pounds leg of lamb, cut into 1" cubes, fat and sinew trimmed

Kosher salt and freshly ground black pepper

1¼ cups minced onions

2 tablespoons finely chopped fresh sage

1 fresh rosemary sprig

2 garlic cloves, crushed

About 2 cups Easter Broth (page 8), chicken broth, or water

½ cup plus 1 tablespoon fresh lemon juice

2 eggs

Heat the oil in a large skillet over high heat. Working in batches if necessary to avoid crowding the pan, add the lamb, season with salt and pepper, and brown on all sides, about 5 minutes.

Add the onions, sage, rosemary, and garlic to the meat and stir to distribute. Lower the heat a little and cook, stirring occasionally, until the juices released by the meat have evaporated and the pan is once again dry, about 12 minutes.

Add 1 cup broth or water and cook, stirring frequently to prevent the meat and onions from sticking and burning. Simmer until the pan is dry, about 7 minutes. Add another cup of liquid and again cook, stirring often, until the pan is dry. Taste the meat. If the meat is still tough, add a little more broth or water and simmer the meat until it is tender and the pan is almost dry.

When the lamb is tender and the onions have mostly melted into the sauce, add ½ cup lemon juice. Mix well and turn off the heat. The residual heat in the pan will cause the lemon juice to boil and reduce to a glaze.

Beat the eggs with the remaining 1 tablespoon lemon juice. Season with salt and pepper.

Wait just until the lamb cools enough so it is steaming less violently, about 3 minutes, stirring it occasionally so it cools evenly. Stir the egg mixture into the fricassee with a rubber spatula. Stir continuously until the eggs begin to thicken the sauce, about 2 minutes. Adjust the seasoning with salt and pepper and serve.

The last stage of this recipe can be a little tricky. If the pan is too hot when you add the eggs, they will scramble, which is not what you want. But you do need some heat or the eggs won't cook. My best advice is to watch the steam coming out of the pan and let that be your guide; you want some but not much.

pan-roasted lamb loin chops with lemons and olives

SERVES 4

The thing to take away from this recipe is a really great way to cook all tender high-quality meat, including loins of beef, pork, or lamb and steaks as well as veal and pork chops.

Look for prime loin chops cut about 2" thick. The way to get the best flavor is to cook them low and slow—you'll get the meat a perfect medium-rare through and through. I add lemons and olives, and I think Salsa Verde (page 255) goes very nicely here.

8 lamb loin chops, each 1½" to 2" thick

Kosher salt and freshly ground black pepper

2 tablespoons extra virgin olive oil plus additional for serving

2 unpeeled garlic cloves, crushed with the back of a knife

4 thick lemon slices

Pinch of sugar

2 large bushy fresh thyme sprigs

30 pitted niçoise olives

Season the lamb very generously with salt and pepper. Heat a large skillet (big enough to hold the chops with some room to spare) over high heat. Add the oil and, when it slides easily across the pan, add the lamb chops, balancing each on the thickest part of the fatty edge. Reduce the heat to medium and brown the fat, about 3 minutes.

Discard the excess fat and turn the chops, meat side down. Cook at a nice even sizzle for 3 minutes.

Flip the chops over. Add the garlic and lemon slices and season with salt and sugar. Cook the lemon slices until they soften and begin to brown, 2 minutes, then flip them. Cook 1 minute more.

If you're nervous about whether your meat is done, you can check it with a meat thermometer. A rare lamb chop will register 120° to 125°F on an instant-read thermometer; medium-rare between 130° and 135°F; and medium between 140° and 145°F.

Bruise the thyme with the back of a kitchen spoon and add it and the olives to the skillet. Cook, basting the meat with the pan juices, about 1 minute more for medium-rare. Remove the pan from the heat, cover it loosely with foil, and allow the lamb to rest for 6 minutes. Arrange the chops on plates, season with salt and pepper, garnish with the olives and lemon, and drizzle with additional oil if desired.

roasted leg of lamb

SERVES 8

The goal with a roasted leg of lamb is juicy meat with a rich brown crust. Begin by studding the lamb with garlic and rosemary, rub the whole thing with olive oil, and then season it generously with salt and pepper. When you are ready to roast, start the lamb in a hot oven (450°F) to caramelize the surface, then reduce the temperature (325°F) and cook the meat through more gently. This two-temperature approach works well for all large roasts—lamb, beef, pork, and even venison.

> 1 leg of lamb (6 pounds), excess fat trimmed, leaving just a thin layer
>
> 2 garlic cloves, peeled and cut into thin slivers
>
> 2–3 fresh rosemary sprigs, broken into short florets
>
> ¼ cup extra virgin olive oil
>
> Kosher salt and freshly ground black pepper

With the point of a paring knife, make incisions about 1" deep all over the lamb. Insert garlic slivers and rosemary leaves into the incisions. Place the meat in a roasting pan. Pour the oil over the lamb and season generously with salt and pepper, rubbing to make sure the oil and seasonings are evenly distributed. Allow the lamb to marinate at room temperature for about 1 hour.

Preheat the oven to 450°F. Roast the lamb for 30 minutes, then lower the heat to 325°F. Continue roasting the lamb until a meat thermometer registers 125°F (for rare to medium-rare; cook the meat longer if you prefer your meat more well done), about 1 hour.

Remove the lamb from the oven and allow it to rest for 20 minutes. Slice the meat and serve dressed with the pan juices.

If you want to roast potatoes with the lamb, cut them in half or into quarters and add them to the pan when you reduce the heat. Season them with salt and pepper and turn them with a spoon after about 40 minutes so they cook evenly.

Once the meat is browned at high temperature, you can figure that it will need to cook 10 minutes per pound for rare to medium-rare, 15 minutes per pound for medium, and 20 minutes per pound for well done. Extremely large pieces of meat, over 8 pounds, will need a minute or two more per pound.

roasted pork with sage, rosemary, and garlic

SERVES 4

Pork loin is a lean, mild cut of meat. I like to add flavor and keep it moist by stuffing it with a mixture of chopped herbs and garlic. Simply make a small channel in the center of the loin with a knife, then poke the stuffing in. The meat will be flavored and basted from within while it roasts.

- 1 boneless pork loin (about 2 pounds)
- 1½ teaspoons chopped fresh sage plus 2 sprigs
- 1½ teaspoons chopped fresh rosemary plus 2 sprigs
- 1 teaspoon minced garlic plus 2 cloves, peeled and lightly crushed
- 3 tablespoons extra virgin olive oil
- Kosher salt and freshly ground black pepper
- Sea salt

Preheat the oven to 375°F. Using a long knife with a thin blade or a clean sharpening steel, make a channel lengthwise through the center of the loin running from one end to the other.

Mix the chopped sage and rosemary in a small bowl. Add the minced garlic and 1 tablespoon oil. Season the mixture with salt and pepper, then poke it through the channel in the meat (I find it easiest to work from both ends more or less at once).

Season the outside of the loin generously with salt and pepper. Heat 2 tablespoons oil over medium-high heat in an ovenproof skillet large enough to hold the loin. Brown the meat on all sides and on each end, about 8 minutes in all.

Add the herb sprigs and crushed garlic to the pan and put it in the oven. Roast for 15 minutes, then turn the loin and roast 15 minutes more, basting from time to time with the pan drippings.

Remove the pan from the oven, cover with foil, and set aside in a warm place for 15 minutes to rest the meat. To serve, cut the loin into generous slices, season with sea salt, and drizzle with the pan juices.

If you are roasting a larger, thicker loin, make two channels through the meat so the seasoning can be better distributed. Cook the loin longer.

If you want, you can use a meat thermometer to check the temperature. I prefer pork cooked so it's still a little pink at the center. You can expect a reading before the final resting of about 135°F. If you like your pork more thoroughly cooked, cook it until the internal temperature reaches 150°F.

desserts

I really make only a few desserts. Like many Italians, I grew up ending a meal with fruit and maybe biscotti, so I never really felt the urge to delve deeply into the pastry kitchen. But I love a good sweet, so although I may not have a particularly large repertoire, I think my small, very traditional battery of desserts is worth sharing.

When I bake, I do it with the same spirit and mindfulness of my ingredients as when I cook. Sugar is a strong flavor, and it's important not to use it as a mask. If you're making a pear tart, you want the pears to taste sweet yes, but mostly you want them to taste like pears. You want to focus on the texture of your crust, think about whether it is meant to be light and flaky or dense and crumbly or somewhere in between, think about working the dough just enough to combine the ingredients, not so much that you activate the gluten in the flour and make it chewy—unless it is supposed to be.

These are simple desserts. They are sweet and tasty, a reflection of generations of refinements. Follow the recipes, but also adapt them. I'm going to stop short of saying you should add sugar to taste, but you should consider balancing the role it plays with the aim of creating a harmonious dish, rather than automatically assuming sugar should receive a starring role.

almond biscotti

MAKES ABOUT 32

Both my mom and I grew up eating these cookies. They are not hard to make and, best of all, last for days.

I use skin-on almonds. It's tedious splitting them all. Skinless almonds, which are easy to buy already halved, will of course work, but I like the color, flavor, and texture the skins add.

½ cup whole skin-on almonds

5 tablespoons plus 1 teaspoon unsalted butter, at room temperature

¾ cup sugar

2 eggs

1 teaspoon vanilla extract

2 teaspoons freshly grated orange zest

2¼ cups all-purpose flour

1½ teaspoons baking powder

⅛ teaspoon freshly grated nutmeg

¼ teaspoon kosher salt

Preheat the oven to 325°F. Grease a baking sheet. Cut the almonds in half and reserve them. Combine the butter and sugar with a mixer (use the paddle attachment) or by hand with a pastry blender. Mix in the eggs, vanilla, and orange zest.

In a separate bowl, combine the flour, baking powder, nutmeg, and salt and mix well. Add the flour mixture to the butter mixture and mix until the ingredients come together. Mix in the nuts by hand, one-third at a time.

Divide the dough in half. On a floured work surface, form each half into a log about 12" long. Put the dough logs on the prepared baking sheet and flatten the top of each with your hands. Bake until the dough begins to color, about 25 minutes.

Allow the dough to cool for about 10 minutes and then slice each log on the diagonal into ¾"-thick biscotti. Arrange the biscotti, cut side down, on a dry baking sheet and toast in the oven until they are nicely browned, about 10 minutes. Cool and serve.

torta di riso

This is a classic Italian sweet from Pisa. For the unfamiliar, it's essentially a rice pudding tart. But that description is not at all sufficient to describe this rich, slightly exotic dessert flavored with dried fruit, sweet spices, and pine nuts. This chocolate version is my favorite. The raisins in the filling are soaked in Italian herbal liqueur, either Strega or Galliano. Strega can be hard to find; but Galliano is easier.

FOR THE CRUST:

½ cup (1 stick) unsalted butter, at room temperature

½ cup sugar

2 eggs

½ teaspoon vanilla extract

2 cups all-purpose flour

1 teaspoon baking powder

Pinch of kosher salt

FOR THE RICE:

1 cup Arborio rice

2 cups whole milk

½ cup sugar

2½ ounces semisweet chocolate, chopped

FOR THE CUSTARD:

¼ cup golden raisins

3 tablespoons Strega or Galliano liqueur

2 eggs

½ cup unsweetened cocoa powder

1 teaspoon vanilla extract

¼ cup diced candied citron

½ cup pine nuts

Grated zest of 1 lemon

Pinch of freshly grated nutmeg

TO MAKE THE CRUST: Combine the butter and sugar with an electric mixer (use the paddle attachment) or by hand with a pastry cutter. Mix in the eggs and vanilla.

In a separate bowl, combine the flour, baking powder, and salt. Add the flour mixture to the butter mixture. Mix until the dough begins to come together and then knead it just until it is smooth. Wrap the dough in plastic and refrigerate for at least 1 hour.

Roll the dough out about ⅛" thick and fit it into a 9" pie plate. Trim the edges, cover the crust with plastic, and chill thoroughly.

TO MAKE THE RICE: Combine the rice, milk, and sugar in a saucepan and bring to a simmer over medium-high heat, stirring occasionally. Reduce the heat to low, cover the pan, and cook until the rice is tender and the milk is absorbed, about 10 minutes. Stir the chocolate into the rice. Stir until the chocolate melts and mixes with the rice, then set the pan aside to cool.

TO MAKE THE CUSTARD: While the rice cooks, soak the raisins in enough liqueur to cover in a small bowl. Soak them until they are soft and absorb the liqueur, about 10 minutes. Once the rice is at room temperature, mix in the eggs, cocoa, vanilla, citron, pine nuts, lemon zest, and nutmeg. Stir in the soaked raisins.

Preheat the oven to 350°F. Spoon the filling into the chilled crust. Smooth the top. Bake the torta until the filling firms and the crust is golden, about 1 hour. Serve at room temperature.

peach tart

SERVES 8

It's the tenderness and lightness of this crust that makes this tart my favorite. The secret to success: Don't overwork the dough. Mix the ingredients only enough to combine them and let the dough rest in the refrigerator before you roll it out.

½ cup (1 stick) unsalted butter

⅓ cup granulated sugar

2 eggs

1 teaspoon vanilla extract

2 cups all-purpose flour

1 teaspoon baking powder

¼ teaspoon kosher salt

¼ cup apricot jam

5 peaches

1 tablespoon fresh lemon juice

About 2 tablespoons confectioners' sugar

This tart is also very good made with pears instead of peaches.

Combine the butter and granulated sugar in a large mixing bowl or with an electric mixer. Incorporate the eggs, one at a time, and then mix in the vanilla.

In a separate bowl, combine the flour, baking powder, and salt; mix well. Add the flour mixture to the butter mixture. Mix only until everything comes together. Form the dough into a ball, wrap it in plastic, and refrigerate for at least 1 hour.

Preheat the oven to 350°F. Butter an 11" tart pan with a removable bottom. Roll the dough out on a floured surface until it's about ¼" thick. Fit the dough into the pan and trim the edges. Spread a layer of jam over the bottom of the tart shell.

I like the subtle glaze you get here by sprinkling the peaches with confectioners' sugar as soon as the tart comes out of the oven. It's a simple thing, but it makes the flavor of the fruit pop.

Pit and quarter the peaches. Slice them lengthwise about ¼" thick. Sprinkle the slices with lemon juice and then arrange them in concentric circles in the tart shell. Bake the tart until the crust is golden, about 30 minutes. Remove the tart from the oven, sprinkle it with confectioners' sugar, and serve warm or at room temperature.

roasted amaretti-stuffed pears

SERVES 4

Amaretti cookies are widely available at gourmet shops and Italian groceries. They are the perfect almond-flavored counterpoint to sweet roasted pears. If you do have trouble finding the cookies, you can order them by mail.

12 amaretti cookies

2 tablespoons pear brandy or almond-flavored liqueur

1 egg yolk

2 tablespoons brown sugar

Grated zest and juice of 1 lemon

3 tablespoons unsalted butter, at room temperature

2 Anjou pears

½ cup port wine or brandy

1 pint vanilla ice cream, for serving

Preheat the oven to 350°F. Crumble the cookies and put them in a large bowl. Add the pear brandy or liqueur and mix, allowing the cookie crumbs to absorb the liquid. Add the egg yolk, brown sugar, lemon zest, and softened butter to the cookies and mix well.

Peel the pears, cut them in half, scoop out the seeds, and coat the pears with lemon juice (so they don't brown). Put the pears, cored side up, in a shallow baking dish, then spoon some of the amaretti stuffing into the hollow in each. Pour the port wine or brandy into the bottom of the dish. Bake the pears uncovered until they are tender, about 35 minutes. Serve warm with a scoop of vanilla ice cream.

buttermilk panna cotta

SERVES 6

Always make panna cotta a day ahead. That way, you are sure to have enough time for it to chill thoroughly and set. In this recipe, buttermilk replaces some of the traditional cream. I like the way the tangy tartness of the buttermilk offsets the richness of the cream.

2 cups heavy cream

1 scant teaspoon powdered gelatin

¼ cup plus 2 tablespoons sugar

1¼ cups buttermilk

Juice of 1 lemon

Put ¼ cup cream in a small bowl. Sprinkle the gelatin over the cream and set it aside to "bloom" (soften) for 5 minutes.

Combine the remaining 1¾ cups cream and the sugar in a saucepan and bring to a boil over high heat, stirring occasionally. Whisk in the buttermilk, lemon juice, and softened gelatin. Pour the panna cotta base through a fine sieve and into six 6-ounce ramekins. Cover with plastic and refrigerate overnight. Serve chilled.

Instead of using buttermilk, consider making panna cotta with a full 3¼ cups of cream but steeping in a flavor before you add the gelatin. You might try chocolate, Earl Grey tea, or cardamom.

pantry

polenta

MAKES ABOUT 6 CUPS

Outside of Italy, polenta hasn't gotten the love it deserves. Soft polenta is a great first course flavored with butter and cheese, and it's the perfect accompaniment to braised or roasted meat and poultry, not to mention meatballs. You can vary the consistency—this is medium soft. If you want it looser or firmer, add more or less liquid. But that's only the beginning. Spread the polenta out on a baking sheet and let it cool and you can slice it and fry it, grill it, or bake it—with or without a filling. No matter how you plan to use it, I recommend you start with coarse ground cornmeal—the texture is more interesting.

Here the polenta is made with water, but you can substitute milk or broth if you want a richer flavor.

6½ cups water

1 tablespoon kosher salt

2 cups coarse ground cornmeal

Be sure to whisk continuously as you add the grain to the liquid so you don't get lumps.

Bring the water to a boil in a large pot over high heat. Add the salt and reduce the heat so the water is just barely simmering. Put the cornmeal in a measuring cup with a spout. Begin pouring it into the water in a slow steady stream while whisking continuously. Whisk until all the cornmeal has been added. Cook the polenta over low heat, stirring occasionally with a wooden spoon, until it begins to pull away from the sides of the pot, about 20 minutes. At this point, you can add butter and freshly grated Parmigiano and, if you like, a little chopped rosemary and serve. Or you can spread the polenta on a baking sheet to cool to slice and cook later.

salsa verde

MAKES ABOUT ¾ CUP

*This condiment is the workhorse of the Italian table. Americans love their
ketchup; an Italian suffers without salsa verde. Everything is better dipped
into this sauce: roasted, poached, or boiled meats and fish, raw vegetables,
and toasted bread. Put it on sandwiches and stir it into pasta—it's all good.
You want it to taste bright and herbal but also briny and sharp—so vary
the amount of each ingredient to get what you're looking for. And be sure
to whisk the sauce vigorously when you add the oil—salsa verde should be
emulsified.*

2½ tablespoons finely chopped fresh flat-leaf parsley

2 tablespoons drained capers

6 anchovy fillets, minced

½ teaspoon minced garlic

½ teaspoon Dijon mustard

About ½ teaspoon red wine vinegar or 1 tablespoon fresh lemon juice

Kosher salt

½ cup extra virgin olive oil

*The general rule is: Use
lemon juice rather than
vinegar if you are mak-
ing the sauce to serve
with fish.*

Put the parsley, capers, anchovies, garlic, mustard, and vinegar or lemon juice
in a bowl and mix well. Add a little salt, then whisk in the oil. Serve at room
temperature.

maionese

MAKES ABOUT 1¼ CUPS

Maionese is no more like commercial mayonnaise than a Ford is like a Lamborghini. Maionese is an elegant sauce. It's also the starting place for classic preparations like aioli and great dishes like Vitello Tonnato (page 228). Making maionese is not hard, but a few tips can help. Begin by letting the eggs warm to room temperature—yolks absorb oil better when they're not cold. Then gather your equipment. I like to fit a metal bowl inside a pot lined with a towel. This keeps the bowl still so I don't need to hold it while I whisk. Get a flexible wire whisk—a stiff one won't work. Incorporate the oil very slowly, whisking all the time. Setting things up right at the beginning really helps.

> 2 egg yolks
> 1½ cups extra virgin olive oil
> Juice of ½ lemon
> Kosher salt and freshly ground black pepper

If you have a squeeze bottle, put the oil in the bottle; if not, put it in a measuring cup with a spout.

Whisk the egg yolks in a metal bowl until they are frothy. Begin to add oil slowly, dribbling it in while whisking continuously.

When the maionese begins to look about as thick as pancake batter and you have added about ¼ cup of the oil, whisk in the lemon juice and a little salt and pepper.

Continue to incorporate the rest of the oil gradually. Adjust the seasoning with salt, pepper, and additional lemon juice if desired. Refrigerate until ready to use. Maionese will keep in the refrigerator for about a week.

lemon confit

MAKES ABOUT 1 QUART

Lemon confit, thinly sliced lemons preserved and flavored in a mixture of salt and sugar, is a restaurant kitchen pantry staple that's equally useful to have in your refrigerator at home. Tangy more than sour and a little briny, preserved lemon adds acid and brightness to Fried Oysters with Shaved Fennel and Aioli (page 159). Preserved lemon is also good chopped and added to sandwiches and salads and stirred into braises shortly before serving. I use slices to flavor steamed fish and veggies and as a garnish for cured meat and fish—like I said, it's useful to have on hand.

6 lemons

2 shallots, peeled and minced

3 garlic cloves, peeled and minced

⅓ cup kosher salt

3 tablespoons sugar

Extra virgin olive oil

Drop the lemons into boiling water for a minute, drain, wipe clean, and then slice thinly. Discard the ends and remove and discard the seeds.

Combine the shallots and garlic in a small bowl. In a separate bowl, mix the salt with the sugar. Put a layer of lemon slices on the bottom of a plastic lidded container. Sprinkle the lemons first with a little shallot mixture, then with some salt mixture. Repeat, layering lemons and sprinkling them with the shallot and salt mixtures until the final lemon slices are topped with the last of the shallots and salt. Cover and refrigerate for 3 days.

The confit is ready to be used at this point. Or cover it with olive oil and keep in the refrigerator for up to a month.

pickled cipollini onions

MAKES 1 POUND

A pantry stocked with pickles is well filled. By pickles, I don't only mean kosher dills. Almost any vegetable is amenable to this age-old treatment, first valued for its power to preserve but quickly loved for the distinctive, and to me addictive, taste. Pickled Cipollini Onions are a traditional pickle. They can be held in the marinade indefinitely, either in a sealed sterile jar, like my mother does, or in the refrigerator, as I do. Either way, they last longer than it takes to use them. Pour the same marinade over cauliflower, green beans, peppers—whatever is fresh—and you have an ingredient that will enable you to make your cooking more complex without much extra work. Use in salads, on sandwiches, and as garnishes.

> 1 pound cipollini onions, peeled
> 3 cups water
> ¼ cup sugar
> 2 tablespoons kosher salt
> 2 garlic cloves, peeled
> 1 teaspoon black peppercorns
> 1 teaspoon fennel seeds
> 1 teaspoon coriander seeds

Put the onions in a large bowl. Combine the water, sugar, salt, garlic, peppercorns, fennel seeds, and coriander seeds in a saucepan. Bring to a boil over high heat. Stir once or twice to make sure the sugar and salt have dissolved, then pour the pickling liquid over the onions. Allow the onions to cool to room temperature and then transfer the onions and liquid to one or more covered containers. Refrigerate for at least 48 hours before using.

acknowledgments

there's no way around starting a list of thank-you's without acknowledging my mom, who first instilled in me a love of cooking. Homegrown, wholesome, and delicious slow food was a part of my life from the beginning, and the kitchen and dinner table were always the center of our home. Growing up in this kind of environment has everything to do with where I am today as a chef, a father, and a husband.

My aunt, Zia Leda, is another major influence. Her garden was a thing of beauty, and the vegetable soups that garden produced are some of the best things I've tasted to this day. I always long for her cooking and constantly find myself calling her for advice; she is a rock star in my eyes.

A huge thank-you to my wife, Amanda, who has always been thoughtful and supportive and has taught our daughter to appreciate the importance of family, healthy food, and delicious cooking. Without her insights and guidance, this book would have been a confusing jumble.

I very much doubt that I would be where I am today without the help and inspiration of my mentor and friend Tom Colicchio. He took me under his wing when I was a complete novice and taught me everything there was to know about the multifaceted world of New York restaurants, taking time to answer my many questions no matter how busy he was.

A thank-you to all of my investors for believing in me and to my partner, Paul Grieco, for keeping the service and beverage programs at our restaurants so on point and interesting—and also putting up with my sometimes irrational Italian temper.

I am incredibly grateful for all the hard-working staff at Insieme, Hearth, and Terroir, especially Jordan Frosolone, Brian Hunt, Dana Gerson, and Jessica Knik for keeping their standards high. I also want to extend my gratitude to all the people who have cooked with me and kept me laughing and learning, especially Jonathan Benno, Ahktar Newab, James Tracy, Damon Wise, and Edward Carew.

My food could not be what it is without the hard work of the farmers and purveyors who provide me with wonderful ingredients every day.

Lastly, this book would not be a reality if it weren't for my friend, cowriter, and recipe tester, Cathy Young; my super agent, David Black; my editor, Pam Krauss and her team at Rodale; John Kernick and Suzie . . . for such beautiful photos; and finally to all of the regular and not-so-regular guests who have supported my restaurants over the years.

index

Underscored page references indicate boxed text and tables. **Boldface** references indicate photographs.